Sensual Voices

True Stories by Women Exploring Connection and Desire

Heal My Voice, Inc
Santa Monica, California

Sensual Voices: True Stories by Women
Exploring Connection and Desire

Published by:
Heal My Voice, Inc
Andrea Hylen
Santa Monica, CA 90401
www.healmyvoice.org

ISBN-13: 978-0692452936 (Heal My Voice)
ISBN-10: 0692452931

Editors: Andrea Hylen,
Marie Ek Lipanovska, Kristina Lovén
Cover design: Karen Brand
Photo Credit: Louise Weibull

Printed in the United States of America

A portion of the proceeds from the sale of this book will
be donated to further the non-profit work of Heal My
Voice.

Dedication

To the writers:

Thank you for your willingness
to share a story with
vulnerability, wisdom, power
and courage.

To the readers:

We honor your journey, your
voice and your heart.

We encourage you to write your
story now.

We are listening.

Blessing

Come, Sit

Hands detect a tender spot
Slowly they inquire
What are you?
What treasures await
In this tender spot?

Memories, stories unfold
Like a rose
Petal by petal
By petal
By petal
Revealing the fragrant gems
Stored in the center

Ah, sweet openings
Into you

Come, Sit
Right here, next to me
I have stories to share
All you need to do is listen

You will see, all will be revealed
You will be revealed

Come, Sit
Right here, next to me
Just listen
The rest will unfold

- Laurel Lozzi

Laurel Lozzi is an eclectic, creative embellisher of this world. She works as a Sex and Desire Coach, awakening sensuality and spirituality through one on one consultation. She is said to declutter closets, bodie,s as well as minds with her exceptional organizational, massage, and coaching skills. Currently she is traveling through Central America, exploring her own emotions and desires and following the guidance of her intuition. Find out more about her at :
www.ToTheOneThatBreathesMe.com
and www.flickr.com/people/laurellozzi/ or you can contact her directly at laurel.lozzi@gmail.com.

TABLE OF CONTENTS

Part One: I AM LONGING

Part Two: I AM Shifting

Part Three: I AM Surrender

Part Four: I AM Sensation

Part Five: I AM Loved

Lisa Hall

Mary K. Baxter
Cassandra Herbert
Ellen Koronet
Marie Ek Lipanovska
Monisha Mittal
Karen Porter
Amber Scott

Jamie Dee Schiffer
Beth Terrence
Kathleen Nelson Troyer

FOREWORD

Brig Feltus

I have been procrastinating writing this Foreword for weeks now. When invited to do it, I felt honored, privileged, and a bit overwhelmed at the prospect of writing about myself. People don't typically see me that way. Nobody expects me to ever feel overwhelmed or flustered. You see, I am a powerful woman. Every space I move through is shifted by my presence. My powers of empathy and compassion are remarkable, and I have strong intuitive gifts. I am charismatic and I have a natural proclivity for making people feel better than they did before crossing my path. I share this up front because my most valued lesson learned in recent times is that vulnerability is the most powerful tool I have in life.

Through vulnerability the world around us reacts to serve the true essence of who we are. It has taken many years and a lot of work to get to this place where I am able to see this clearly and demonstrate it in my everyday life.

I started a practice over the last year that is grounded in the phrase, "I have everything I want". For most people this statement is a romantic notion that sounds good but is totally impractical in application. For some it even sounds arrogant. Well, that's not what's behind it. It's actually a very spiritual statement about everything being possible and that everything that is for me is already for me and awaiting my choosing to receive it. I am really committed to the idea of being unreasonable, you see.

So yes, I am practicing having everything I want. The trick is that I am not referring to surface wants. I'm referring to what my higher self, my inner beast, my uninhibited master desires. That's what I'm committed to. And it actually works. I have everything I want. There is no more powerful statement an individual can make. And vulnerability, it turns out, is key. To get to those inner desires I had to peel back all those layers of programming and reveal my true self. I had to then acknowledge my desires, and then choose to be the woman I needed to be in order to make that one statement, "I have everything I want" true.

So here I am. My desire right now is to introduce you to this incredible opportunity to receive inspiration, motivation, and movement through the incredible stories of these extraordinary women. If you are reading this foreword, your time has come. A portal is opening. You are being beckoned to cross the threshold. Will you answer the call? Will you open yourself to be vulnerable enough to receive the incredible wealth of life experience found herein?

I trust you will.

Brig Feltus: Los Angeles native, poet, lifecoach, activist, singer, songwriter, Brig grew up on a farm in Compton, California. She has spent her life learning to defy modern social paradigms regarding age, sex, and paths to mastery. She started as a Vidal Sassoon-trained makeup artist/hairstylist for high fashion and feature film, shown in publications such as Vogue Italia, and for clients such as Roberto Cavalli, Cartier and Chanel. Ms. Feltus is founder of The Goddess Tribe and a diversity ambassador for One Taste. She is a sought after speaker on the topic of empowerment and freedom of expression. In July 2015, Phase One- Unleashed, of her current album project, The Hungry Beast Sessions, will release.

http://www.brigfeltus.com/
https://twitter.com/brigfeltus

Introduction

Andrea Hylen

Founder of Heal My Voice

In college, I studied Human Sexuality as part of my Social Work degree from Temple University. Reading the book, "Our Bodies, Ourselves," written by the Boston Women's Health Collective was the first time I can remember hearing the voices of women sharing their experiences with vulnerability and information about a woman's body. One evening, I sat in a woman's circle where every woman was handed a plastic speculum, a mirror, a flashlight and lubrication. We were taught how to do the breast exam and pelvic exam on ourselves. All of the women took off their pants and underwear, lay down on blankets and pillows and prepared to follow the step-by-step instructions to touch and examine our own bodies. I remember the exclamations of awe and joy and tears when a woman saw her cervix for the first time. Women empowering women in a circle gathering. That was 1978 and I was 22 years old.

During the late 90's, I taught medical students at Johns Hopkins University how to do the pelvic and breast exam first with words and instructions. Then I gave each of them a hands-on-experience, using my body as a practice patient. Dressed in a hospital gown, I taught them how to hold and use the speculum, guiding their hands to insert the speculum into my vagina with me as their first patient. I talked about the importance of creating a safe environment and using a gentle touch to preserve each woman's dignity. In five years of teaching, I had over 500 pelvic and breast exams with 500 different medical students.

In 2013, I entered a new experience with my body when I was introduced to a 15 minute partnered practice called Orgasmic Meditation (OM). In this partnered practice with a man, I experienced the potential for us to heal our sexuality through better communication, attention and connection. No goal. 15 minutes of connection, sensation and the awakening of desire. I practiced OM with multiple partners in a safe community environment and learned how to teach the technique by taking courses with a company called OneTaste. I have now taught individuals and partners around the world how to practice Orgasmic Meditation.

All of these experiences have led to this book project called Sensual Voices. My deepest desire has been for women to have a place to connect, have conversations, share vulnerability and support each other. This 9th Heal My Voice/Heal My Voice Sweden collaboration has been a place for women to have conversations about the body and write about their own experience of sensuality, connection and desire.

*****

In the beginning of launching Sensual Voices as a program, there were challenges to finding women who would sign up to participate. Sensuality as a topic was not embraced by the masses and there was a point where I only had a few women enrolled in the program. We needed 20-25 participants to make it a viable group and to support it energetically and financially. I might have given up except for three things:

1. I was living in a community house in Venice, California with ten people and I had "permission and encouragement" to talk about sensuality, power,

sexuality and desire. Any time of the day and night. Breakfast, lunch and dinner.

2. A dear friend, Roberta Creeron told me it was an important topic to write about, talk about and make visible in the world. She said, "You have to do it and you have to do it now!" A few hours later Roberta died suddenly and unexpectedly from an abdominal aneurysm.

3. I took a six-week trip to Sweden where I stayed with Marie Ek Lipanovska, founder of Heal My Voice Sweden who had the same desire and the same idea for a book topic. We decided to collaborate on this project and create a bridge between Sweden and the United States.

Thank you Marie. Thank you Roberta. Thank you dear Venice House community.

We finally found the twenty women who were ready to dive into this topic and go on a journey of exploration; Twelve women from Sweden; eight women from the United States with co-facilitators from Sweden and the U.S. We gathered in a secret Facebook group and stoked the fires to stir up the burning embers of desire, connection and sensuality hidden within our souls. We explored universal experiences of a woman's body. Menstruation. Childbirth. Menopause. Sexual Desire and Trauma. We discussed body sensations of sensuality, power, grief, abandonment, life and death with courage and vulnerability. Our experiences included writing and speaking, healing, reclaiming power tied up in an old story, connection with community, intentional space, deep listening and at the end of the process, clarity around the next step in leadership. It also involved the willingness to have conversations about how this particular topic was connected to our lives.

*****

When we started to write, I thought I was ready, really ready, to reveal my own journey. It wasn't until I began to write my personal story I felt a new vulnerability and resistance to writing and exposing my story even to myself. I found my hands hovering over the computer keyboard afraid to write anything. I had a flood of fearful thoughts: Can I really tell this story? How will it affect my business? Will Heal My Voice lose all credibility if I write a sensual story about desire and sex? Can I really write about looking at Playboy magazines when I was 11 years old? Can I write about the desire to have sex now that I am 58 years old and a widow, a mother, a grandmother? Can I write about the sensuality essence that is waking up in me? I had to walk my own path by diving in over and over to write my own story.

This is the ninth personal story I have written in a Heal My Voice/Heal My Voice Sweden book program and it is the first time I was afraid to put my words onto paper even in the privacy of my home. And that was a clue that I am not the only woman who feels vulnerable to admit my desires, embrace the sensations and to have open conversations. I knew I had to write a story about Sensuality that connected to my Sexuality.

It was the women in this community of co-authors who read the drafts of my story, who acknowledged my courage and who told me to just write the story without the need for approval and without justifying why I felt the need to write it now. Each woman was held with the same love, care and encouragement. And as each woman completed her story, it opened the door for the next woman to keep writing and complete her story. We held each other, shared our voices, one word at a time, until twenty stories were completed. We are in this together…

You must do the things you think you cannot do.
~Eleanor Roosevelt

I invite you to open yourself to a new perspective as you read the stories and ask yourself some questions.

*What if we could spread Universal Love by donating energy, money and time to empower women and girls?

*What if women supported each other with parenting tips instead of judging and comparing and competing to be the best parent with the best child?

*What if we opened to the anomalies in life by accepting our unique differences and stopped trying to be carbon copies of each other?

*What if we accepted that relationships could be monogamous, open, dynamic, hetero, homo, bi and we supported each other to love who we love?

*What if we shared our vulnerability, wisdom, and claimed our personal power and inner authority?

*What if we put our ideas together and changed the things that aren't working on the planet, finding new solutions and building the future together?

*What if we allowed ourselves to feel everything and to notice it without making anyone else right or wrong?

As you read the stories in this book, I invite you to listen for your own questions and answers. Close your eyes. Connect with your heart. And randomly open to a story. Go now. Enter the pages and be open to the mystery of what will unfold.

Andrea Hylen believes in the power of a woman's voice to usher in a new world. She is the founder of Heal My Voice, a Writing and Transition Coach and Orgasmic Meditation teacher. Andrea has discovered her unique gifts while parenting three daughters and learning to live life fully after the deaths of her brother, son and husband. She is currently living out of a suitcase following her intuition as she travels around the world speaking, teaching, collaborating and leading workshops. Her passion is authentically living life and supporting others in doing the same.
*www.andreahylen.com **www.healmyvoice.org***

Photo Credit: Wendy Mata

Part One

I Am Longing

"Longing, felt fully, carries us to belonging"

-Tara Branch, Radical Acceptance

Story One

Welcome Beautiful Life

Annaparjata Jasmine Sandström

Surrounded by the white hospital walls I slowly look up after what seems like hours. In dimmed lights that move across my vision field, the contours of my surroundings gradually become clearer. I turn my head to drink, but my body is so tired it is an effort to just receive a small sip of water. Blurry and sore my eyes look around, with a watery surface that blends with a few drops of sweat on my face. I begin to meet the eyes around me. Closest is my boyfriend standing slightly bent over me and giving me a supportive and loving look, with my dedicated midwife and doula in the background.

We have been at the maternity ward for many hours now. I was almost fully open at arrival, but the birthing has not moved forward much since. For a split second, I feel like giving up; and me being a person who has longed for this experience and this baby for so long. Why did it not continue flowing, as it did at home? Would I manage this pain and effort much longer? Would I be able to give birth to our baby?

They are all standing with their heads slightly downward and with a low dispirited gaze on their faces. My heart beats harder. I realize the significance of what is happening and quickly close my eyes again. I have to turn inside again and again to that embracing, comforting sense of Being, as each moment going by grows more and more challenging. There I can find some calm and soothing trust, as the contractions start again. My body is thrown like a cloth being twisted and turned in pulsations of fierce force. I breathe deeply to follow the unrestricted waves of oneness and sharp pain coming and going in a pulsating staccato. But now, after seeing the discouraged eyes around me saying: "*Nobody* knows what to do", my mind begins sending threatening thoughts. I hear them as a stubborn but distant echo as I see the midwife coming closer to me with a needle. She tells me that she has called for the doctor. (In Sweden this only happens during giving birth when there is a medical problem).

The labor pains are at this point becoming weak, my whole body-mind is exhausted, and my baby, although fine on all measures, is still not moving down the last centimeters in the birth canal enough for me to push. The midwife briefly looks at the needle. It is like a foreign threat from a faraway reality that suddenly seems *so* close. I know what the needle contains; a strong medicine to completely stop the labor work, and then a caesarian section would be the only way forward. I see sadness behind her comforting eyes as she sits down to hold my hand with the needle in a steady grip in the other.

In contrast to the stillness and slow motion in my exhausted body, my heart now beats hard and fast. I close my eyes again and turn to my baby. Every labor pain a new meeting with him, letting me know if I need to breathe deeper and how he is doing. Inside, connected with him and in my body, all is okay. It is like a shelter from everything but us working together. No thoughts, no distracting fears, inhibitions or expectations, just us two living this moment together. Then it happens. Like a string *just* before it breaks, my whole body tenses up so totally I break into a scream, a scream of helplessness and of giving in. My body unexpectedly stays in one long contraction that lasts for over 10 minutes instead of the normal 1.5. As the string breaks, I fall like a dry leaf through open space of quiet air and land in a place of soft surrender that at the same time holds me tightly like a pair of big, stable hands.

This moment was essential. I had to acknowledge that I might not be able to give my baby his birth into this world safely held in our connection and love, a bond building over nine months. My heart nearly broke to let it go because that meant that he might have to take the transition into this world all alone. I took a deep breath, opened my hands and concentrated all my attention into the connection between us; deep down in the birth canal and in spirit where we still were together, connected as one. I cried inside in the space of rest between each contraction. But the tears held yet a different truth – that this was also the most beautiful moment of my life.

We are together right *now*, in the most intimate cocreation to bring his little body into this world! He is here! And he is coming out to us now! And I am doing the best I can. I *am doing the best I can.* Surrendering to the incredible arriving of our son in whatever way it will happen suddenly fills my heart with immense gratitude. He responds and sends calm waves to all of my senses, conveying that he is peaceful and warm, safe and at ease. "I am ok mama".

The door opens, and two doctors come in. "But the baby *has* moved down!" the doctor examining me says and looks at me with trustworthy, happy eyes. I look up at my midwife, and I see that she does not believe him. She examines me, and like the brightest glorious sun she lights up: "It's time you bring out the power dear, because now you shall push him out!" Without uttering a word, a twinkle of appreciation in her eyes once again expressed her sweet support; "You have done everything asked of you, here is the reward, now push!"

And so I did.

Like the ocean touching the shore with all its power and love, the labor swayed me in and out of our melting connection – it was me and my baby. And we danced! We met in the most painful, most sensual and most beautiful dance. Together we *were* the ocean *and* the shore. I myself could not do anything at all, and yet, without me, nothing at all would happen. Together as one we can create everything from here to forever and it was so crystal clear in that moment. The ocean will *never* stop kissing the shore, no matter how many times she is sent away. The birthing mother will never stop receiving the waves of opening to her baby, no matter how much it hurts. And babies are born.

Every wave of contraction grew bigger and bigger. Simultaneously the bond between me and my little one intensified. A small voice said, "Wait, wait, wait," until the peak of each contraction for me to reach the precise moment of exactly when to push. Growling deeply like a bear I pushed with every inch of strength I had left.

And at last he came! A gorgeous, strong and lively, baby boy. Our son.

I turn my head down to receive our son. His little voice is deep when he lets out his first loud cry and his breath is strained with liquid. Holy mother, he is like a divine athlete! So strong and beautiful! Like a wild heart of pure love he lands twisting and turning on my chest. To feel his soft little body, see his tiny hands, his feet with ten little toes and his wrinkly sweet face, smell his unique mild scent, and to *love* him – now as a little human being entering our life forever – is an unforgettable feeling of bliss.

The umbilical cord is cut, now we are not one, but two. And instead of the physical connection, I sense an invisible but still so tangible bond of love and protection grow even stronger. As he calms down, we let his wise little body find his way to my breast with one hand to support him. His tender face worms up towards me, bores around into my breast and finally sighs while he takes a firm grip of my nipple. The feeling is indescribable as he takes his first sip of life from my body, and he drinks what feels like a blend of safety, nourishment and love.

We stay at the hospital the following days because my body needs to heal and receive blood. I breastfeed him often and he sucks intensely to get milk. He keeps searching for the breast and takes what I have throughout the days, thus breastfeeding grows more and more painful. And it is almost unbearable to see his attempts to get more when the milk runs out, every time. I begin pumping and nurse him as often as possible, but he does not get enough and on the second day we have to begin giving him little doses of formula.

I have never wanted anything as much as I wanted to meet my baby's need for nursing and resting safely at my breast. For months we tried everything, from nursing all day long to different kinds of strategies to increase the production. But it didn't grow enough to be enough. Continuously we gave him formula so he would be fulfilled. We then found a devise for breastfeeding *with* formula. It means that the bottled milk is on my chest hanging in a band and two tiny tubes bring milk down and into his mouth as he breastfeeds normally. So he drinks formula at the same time as he is breastfeeding. It was supposed to be an effective way of increasing the body's own production of milk, but it also didn't work. Nothing worked, and every time I tried something new I felt so enormously helpless. I had to give in over and over again and deep feelings of sadness and disappointment followed every attempt. Why was my body not working? Was I really doing *everything* I could?

I could not give him the security of breastfeeding spontaneously on every signal. I could not give him the biological goodness of enzyme and antibodies of my breast milk. I could not give him the continuous experience of connection through the special physical closeness of breastfeeding all of his infant life. And I cried, sometimes with my son in my arms, and often when I had a little space to myself. Crying helped me open to feel the overwhelming love I have for him, which was behind the grief. It also helped to keep me coming back to a happy heart to connect with my son. It made me see that I really *did* everything I could. And finally, through crying I felt that the core understanding for me to embrace in this experience is that *my love* is enough. Loving him and giving him everything I can is enough. Doing the best I can, being his newborn and sometimes insecure mother, is enough. And the contractions in grieving reached a shore of rest into how the situation was, not how I wished it would be, and I could surrender – returning to the ocean.

Grieving for what I could not give him turned into gratefulness for what I could do, and new possibilities opened. I found energy to continue breastfeeding with the device, nursing him could therefore continue in this unnatural but amazing way. Soon I also came across a mother who had too much breast milk and she wanted to donate the excess to me. She was a new acquaintance whom I met over the internet and she just wanted her milk to come to someone's good. I received it and gave it to him. I believe it was the most loving gift I have ever received and he drank her milk with joy!

The breastfeeding device, never giving up *together* with a willingness of giving in to the limitations of my body *and* a huge amount of perseverance brought me to the feeling that our son *had* been breastfeeding well, while mostly with formula and another woman's milk.

These experiences ended up becoming a precious life lesson; that without the contractions in life, surrender becomes nothing but a passive empty outbreath, and without surrendering to life, the contractions become a clenched fist with no purpose to follow. The ocean and the shore cannot exist without each other. To me this now seems to be the whole – seemingly contradictory – beautiful point of surrender. And none of it would have happened without the loving people around me. Together, we can create life – just like nothing in this world can exist without being in relation to something else, placing Connection as the Essence of Creation. Out of this incredible journey I have come to live a whole new reality; that it is only in connection to my own body, to other dear ones, flowers rivers and trees, animals and to God, that I come truly alive – placing Togetherness as the Essence of Living. And I love living this life with you, my son.

Annaparjata Jasmine Sandström is a psychologist, specialized in the significance of safe human connection for normal early neurobiological development. She embodies the experience of how being in warm trusting relationships accordingly facilitates long-term growth and healing. Her broad knowledge coupled with a well-nurtured sensitivity for these tender human needs makes her a master at creating a feeling of safety for the people she works with. As the mother of a newborn, she joyously lives and breathes this process of wholeness and connection with her child, as well as within herself and in the world. Her life is dedicated to it.
annaparjata@hotmail.se

Story Two

The Road to "Not Lost"

BettyAnn Leeseberg-Lange

Whenever we moved, it was like "pulling up roots", being ripped once again. What I felt? Both anxiety and anticipation!

First came this rush of packing. Dad determined; Mom on the edge of frenzy. She always packed the good dishes and crystal herself, never trusting anyone else – no packer, no dad and certainly no child.

Then Mom crowded all the necessities into the car while Dad complained, "When are we leaving? What is taking so long,

Annemarie? No, we are not taking that!" After we crammed ourselves into the car, Mom announced, ritually, "There, Ralph, we are all in." And off we went.

Traveling was an unbelievably secure time for me. We existed, out of time, just us, the family, in the comfort of that old 1951 dark green Hudson. The inside of "The Car", all grey plush, even the sides. It felt warm and cozy and special. That expensive automobile even had a radio! We listened to it all the way down from Wisconsin to Texas. My Dad got the car second hand, paying much less than it was worth, and we were very proud of it. We had never had so much elegance and all the trappings of wealth. The inside of "The Car" seemed enormous to me. I loved that car! I felt so safe there.

Ralph, my brown-haired baby brother, age 3, sat in the front seat between Mom and Dad, the place of honor. My beautiful blond blue-eyed younger sister, Margaret, age 6, and I pleaded to take turns up there, but to no avail. And wasn't I the redhead with the glasses, age 8, the eldest? Shouldn't I know better than to whine! I think Mom put Butch, my brother's nickname, in the front seat to protect him from his two older, stubborn and troublesome sisters.

There we were with books to read and games to play. We each had our own books, a blanket, and our own special baby pillow. I had mine until I was 28. My beautiful Golden Retriever puppy, Hostage, ate it. I cried for days.

We played card games mostly (they took up less space) until we got bored. Then the arguments began. The complaining happened most often when we were hungry or sleepy. Mom could usually quiet us with graham crackers, which we promptly got all over the seat and had yet again another thing to moan about. Or apple slices which were no better because we got the car seat and walls of the doors sticky, as well as our hands, faces, dresses, and one another.

This caused the terrible wet washcloth, to come out. That thing was kept in aluminum foil wrapped around a sliver of soap for cleaning our faces, hands and the back seat. We hated that washcloth and so much wailing occurred that one of us would end up in the front seat. The place of honor then became the place of punishment because we had to sit between two frowning parents.

When we were both really irritable and had been told to behave and go to sleep, with some very low grumbling, we put our heads on the low arms of the doors. This led to our feet being together so we could kick one another. First came our feet and then our blankets and then our pillows, hitting one another, until Margaret cried. She would always cry. It was exhausting!

Often Mom suggested we divide the back seat. In those days old elegant cars had soft fabric cushions with seams down them and in our car there were an even number of units, much to Mom's relief. So logistically we each had an even space, nothing to fight over, except we were 6 and 8. Sometimes it did work and calmed us down. On the other hand, sometimes it was just another point of contention

One afternoon on an especially long day, I was being quite demanding and stubborn in the back seat, fighting with my sister and then talking back to my Dad. Now, talking back to my Mom would have gotten me a "good talking to". Talking back to my Dad, the Air Force Sergeant, was tantamount to talking back to God. And that's when it happened. My Dad ordered us, in his full sergeant's voice, to stop it or he was going to put the next one who made a sound out of the car. And it was I.

He became so angry that he stopped the car and ordered me out. Mom gave me my coat. She was as annoyed as he was by that time, so she slammed the door shut. And my Dad drove off. They left me there, by the side of the road, next to empty open farmland with a barbed wire fence around the field, gravel next to the road, wet dried out grass and a deep gully with muddy water in it.

It was dark fall. It was cold; the wind blew. It burned my face, blowing my hair into my mouth. My fingers turned all red and numb. I was terrified. I was cold and stunned and stood there for what seemed like a very long time...feeling completely abandoned. And crying, with the tears chilling on my cheeks, the harsh wind streaming them down my face.

And then a little part of me got mad and that part of me tried to figure out what to do next. Stubbornly, I wasn't going to let them have the final say. I remembered that if I stayed on the gravel right next to the grass, facing the traffic, I wouldn't get hit by a car or truck barreling down the narrow two-lane road.

I remembered what my grandfather, the minister, taught me. If you walked far enough around fenced-in land, sooner or later you would come to a farmhouse. There would be a road to that house and a gate and maybe a dog – friendly or unfriendly.

I examined in my mind what would I do in each case. . I recalled seeing a farmhouse just before I was put out of the car. So I began walking back the way we came.

I was terrified, abandoned, and crying so hard. I walked with my heart screaming inside, but a stubborn locked jaw outside. I knew, I just knew, I hoped against the panic that someone would save me. I prayed "Dear God, please, don't leave me … save me … save me…I don't want to die out here without anyone … please, please, please."

And I saw a house on the horizon with the light on the pole. Every farmhouse had one. In case there was some kind of danger in the night, people would know where to go for help. Or they could find a place to sleep against a house or in an open barn or in a corner away from the wind. Sometimes there was a meal if you did some work around the house to earn that meal.

I was saved or would be because I was sure a nice grandma kind of lady would come to the door. She would be so sorry for me that she would take me in. I would live with her and her husband, as they had no children. And I would live happily ever after.

I trudged along working out what I was going to say to the dog and the nice people, who surely would adopt me, and I was going to say, "Nyah, Nyah, Nyah," to my Father. Then I heard a car coming up slowly behind me, honking its horn and my Mother calling out to me, "Betty, Betty".

I watched as my Father grimly, slowly drove up, carefully parking on the other side of the road. I was stunned. I just stood there. I didn't know whether to be glad or sad or mad. My whole scenario changed. I thought they wouldn't come back to get me, that they really wouldn't come back. I had planned for anything else, everything else, or so I thought.

There I was, with my eight-year old plans, and now they were back. My Mother was crying and calling out, as only a distraught mother can, for a lost child. My Father was sitting guiltily at the wheel, trying not to look horrified at what he had done. My sister's little face was pressed against the window, her blue eyes wide as saucers. And my poor baby brother was sitting in the back seat, picking at his "blankie" – blocking out everything he had heard in the car.

At first I really didn't know what to do...I had to rearrange all the plans I made for my life. At that moment I really didn't want to go back. It seemed that whatever lay before me had to be better than being left by the side of the road. I thought my Mother wanted me back, but then why had she let my Father put me out of the car. I sure as hell was not sure about my Father wanting me back. I had been his "Little Red Headed Girl". He would swing me around singing, badly, "Casey would waltz with a Strawberry Blond..." Now I didn't know what to think. I felt so befuddled, so lost, so betrayed.

I decided in my terror of being left alone, to give them another change, to go "home". And I so wanted out of the cold. I never liked the cold. To this day, I am sure Hell is cold, not hot!

I ran across the road to the car, not even looking both ways. As I got to the other side of the car, a huge truck came whizzing by. My Mother pulled me into the car, the front seat and hugged me and hugged me. She rocked me and rocked me, crying and crying - more out of her fear and shock than mine. I was crying too, but not from feeling saved. I was crying because I knew I would never really be safe again. "You will never do that again, Ralph," she said to my Father in the most warning of tones.

I realized it really would never happen again, but I didn't know what would. After a while, my brother got fussy, as 3 year olds do, and I went again into the backseat. I sat in that dear old car, sadly wishing I didn't know what I now knew. I knew there would never be days of innocent trust again. I cried myself to sleep.

And the terror is always there. Yup, not was – is! Whenever I don't know where I am on a road, I become that little eight-year old girl. I still have to talk myself down from the terror. "I will be OK; I have gas in the car; there are information signs; I have my cell phone. I can get off the road at any time, go to the nearest gas station and ask for directions.'

The truth is: I can even get lost in a building. And once again, I have to talk myself out of a panic attack: "There are signs, BettyAnn." "But will people give me directions that I can follow?" "These people will help you, even if they are rude." And eventually, when I get wherever I am going, only then can I relax. I breathe deeply and smile – as if I have won an award!

I remember and am amused at how resourceful that little eight-year old girl was. She remembered what she learned; called out to God for help; made plans for what would happen next – all positive – all forward moving. In fact, I am quite proud of that little girl! And I am proud of me!

And yet, the sadness still exists. I have been told that if I write about such things, they will heal. I wonder. But I know we keep going, scared, yet still walking into the future. The terror comes and goes. And that is how it is! The sea moves toward and away from the shore, as we do in our lives. The road lies in front of us and in back of us. We can go either way; fear exists either way. And I choose the road going forward.

Who knows what triumphs are beyond the fear!

BettyAnn Leeseberg-Lange grew up a military child. *She trained as an actor, working in NYC's theatre, television and film. BettyAnn also coached people to modify their accents, her most famous student being Howard Stern. BettyAnn then taught at Midwestern universities and The Catholic University of America. She dialect coached at DC major theaters, and television, coaching Dominic West and Idris Elba for HBO's series THE WIRE. BettyAnn opened Talking Well Consulting, working with internationals to modify their accents so they are understood, accepted and respected. BettyAnn believes national identity and speech clarity are important, and necessary in our global community.* ***http://talkingwellconsulting.com/***

Story Three

Sparkling Turbulence: The Uncovery

Ellen Koronet

1972. Age 12. There I was in my bright yellow room. I had rearranged the furniture. I loved my couch under the bookshelf that was crowded with my favorite books and games, and my bed by the window with our black cat

Misty curled up on the radiator shelf. I loved my bulletin board with its cut-outs and photos. I loved my desk, where I had everything I needed to dive into 7th grade research reports or study my Spanish. And I loved my secret cove in the back of the long dark closet, under the stairs leading to the third floor.

My usually messy way-too-yellow room was my only refuge from American middle school, where my mismatched clothes were jeered at and my hair never played nice – always falling out of its ponytail and landing in a heavy mess covering my eyes. At school, boys constantly twisted my name (Tachau) into "trashcan" or "tushie" and friendships with girls always seemed to end up in someone's basement, with pressure to pair off with the boys conveniently picked for the occasion.

My room was also a hallway of sorts for my older sister. I never knew when she might knock quickly and then burst through, usually with a scolding: "Why are you still up? You need to turn the lights off right now!" I never thought "do not enter" was an option – my sister needed to get to her room. And I trusted her and I believed her when she said, "I wish Mom had done this for me."

Mom only came to our rooms when she was drawn there by my sister – their fights spilling into my space before Mom retreated. When I think of connecting with Mom, Dad was always right by her side: She was calling us to dinner; or it was a Sunday morning and we all piled onto their big bed. They were playing chamber music in our living room; or we were on vacation, spending hours in the car and then setting up camp or hiking somewhere.

There were two exceptions to this absence of direct conversation: When Mom was beside herself with anger over something I had done or when she was taking a bath and I had a question. In those rare quiet moments, she invited me in, covering her breasts with a washcloth, and we talked softly about things that mattered to me.

The only time Mom and my sister seemed to coordinate their disjointed attempts to guide me came in the form of a book carefully placed at the door to my room when I came home from camp that year. This was the year my bunkmates were exploring sex – talking about it, sharing "facts" about it, speculating about it, and playing all kinds of kissing games with the boys' side of camp. I was squirming under the pressure, longing to be anywhere but in that space. I came home to this clinical book, mocking me as if to say: *"Here, you are a MESS. Just read this and you'll be all straightened out."* What I yearned for was not in the book – I wanted to be reassured, seen, heard, loved right where I was. This was the year I discovered that I could secretly help myself to experience some of the pleasure my peers seemed to be lusting after, without telling a soul. In one buried sentence, the book called me "normal." I shrugged my shoulders and left it at that.

1973. Ankara, Turkey: A reprieve from my room in the middle. For one year, the younger part of our family was split out into a more playful unit. My parents, younger twin brothers and I traveled to Turkey where I attended the English-language classes in "third year middle school," their equivalent of 8th grade. My jam-packed pass-through living space was magically replaced with a penthouse suite. I had my own little sleeping room, just big enough for a small bed, and I had access to the glass-enclosed office at the top of the apartment. Mom was still hiding from me: The tender bathtub conversations became a vague memory. But without my sister to answer to, I began to settle into myself.

On Sunday afternoons, just Dad and I walked through the neighborhood to pick up freshly ground coffee (with me barely tolerating the pungent smell of roasting beans), then across the street to the wine shop, then a car ride down and over to the bakery. I put up with all the early stops on our Sunday missions... It was the bakery I lived for. Dad would let me pick one treat for myself from the lush abundance of lokum (Turkish Delight) and crème brule and baklava. When he allowed me to spend a little more, I picked a fruit tart with pudding and kiwi and strawberry because I loved the colors and textures and it felt so much more exciting than a crumbly biscuit.

In that setting, I discovered that there are people who are born and raised halfway across the world from one another, under completely different religious traditions, who can view Life through the same lens. I did not mind the regimented feel of the uniformed school I attended, for it came with a wonderful new independence: Arm in arm with my new friends, we were allowed to charge through the streets of the city at lunchtime, delighting in the delicious offerings of the street vendors and walk-up windows. With arms locked, I began to feel what it was to be included.

I was 13 years old, just at the age where my hairy legs had become an unintended statement. At the beginning of the year, I gave in to the forceful suggestion of a new friend, an American born Turkish girl with a poster of Donny Osmond on the ceiling over her bed, and I attempted to shave my legs. But, to the horror of this new friend, I stopped at my knees, afraid of cutting myself: The required knee socks of my uniform ended up accentuating my still hairy knees. To avoid even her gentle ridicule, and especially to avoid the bribes offered by boys in exchange for speaking Turkish swearwords, I began to hold myself in a kind of silence.

One night, my parents had guests over for dinner. I excused myself after dinner, as usual. When I discovered a spot of blood in my underwear, I sought Mom out in alarm. In her customary way, she did not make the connection between my age and my gender for me. Hiding her own panic, she scurried out of the room, directing me to wait there. Without warning, one of my parents' dinner guests, a doctor, abruptly entered the bathroom where I stood awkwardly exposed from the waist down. Averting his eyes, he asked if I'd started my period yet, then backed out of the room, advising me only to talk to my mother, and leaving me overwhelmed with shame and confusion.

The invasion of privacy and avoidance of conversation about something so personal seemed natural and familiar to me. And so I felt completely and utterly wrong for having this Problem when guests were over. I took a bath, perhaps seeking out the reassurance of the old bathtub conversations. But instead, I felt like I would never wash the yucky feeling off. I lay there wishing I could just send my breasts right back to wherever they came from along with the unwelcome monthly cycle. No thank you. Not mine.

Towards the end of the year, on a whim one day, I allowed the local salon girls to razor-cut my long, thick hair, and I once again tasted a new kind of freedom. The curls they released felt so soft, light, dancing, and fun. When my parents dropped me off at the security gate of the airport on my way to visit a pen-pal in the Basque region of Spain, I was sporting my newly shortened curly-headed haircut and wearing a black gauze shirt embroidered in gold-colored thread. As I approached the screening station, an official pulled me out of the women's line and gestured me over to the men's line. With my heart in my throat when he wasn't looking, I hesitantly slid back to the women's line. As he began to raise his voice and chatter at me in Turkish, I tried asking for my parents, I tried reasoning but I found myself reduced to uncontrollable shaking. A nun standing behind me stepped forward. She, in her austere nun's habit, dried my tears and convinced the officials that I was in the right place: A young woman passing through security to new adventures.

During that year, I began to trust the messiness of stepping out and pushing through whatever showed up. Like a sunset on turbulent water, the light began to catch, reflecting back in a whole new way.

I found my traveling partner in January of 1986, the moment I took my now-husband's hand to thank him for coming to a party I helped host. It was a New Year's Eve folk-dancing party and the remaining guests and I had invited him to stay overnight in a sleeping bag on my floor. The party spilled over into the morning. The two of us did not pay much attention to each other except to have a pleasant breakfast conversation where we discovered that, at different times and without overlapping, we had each lived in the same town growing up. When it was time for him to leave and I took his hand to say "thank you for coming," I felt a crazy kind of shock that seemed to emanate from his deep brown eyes. In a split-second, that "electricity" surged through my body in what can only be described as a tidal wave of recognition, a sense of belonging and of being Seen. To this day, I wear the diamond he gave me two years later – always catching the light just so, reminding me that, like the fragmented reflections of our experiences, we can always catch the rainbow-colored sparkles if we choose to pay attention.

Ellen Koronet is "Chief Fun Officer" of LNK Creative: designing and hosting quizzes and assessments for "soulful" entrepreneurs. LNK Creative also conducts focus groups, surveys, and provides creativity-based solutions to individuals and teams. "Inner Muse & Inner Mentor Creativity & Inspiration Cards," a photo deck and guidebook, are available at: www.LNKcreative.com/store.

Ms. Koronet is an Applied Anthropologist who has been studying the varied cultures of products and services for large corporations since the early 1980s. She speaks and instructs at prominent conferences and events, including Maryland Women's Business Center, QRCA Conference, On Purpose Women Conferences, Communication Central, and Power Conference. **www.LNKcreative.com**

Story Four

My Love Story

Petra Brynell

I was born with a perfect mind, soul and body. I was born with an inner fire and a sense of feeling that I was the absolute greatest gift to the world. I had a sense of worthiness that comes with that. I was able to let my emotions, fantasy and inspiration flourish like waves. Oh, and how I loved to play. I could play for hours. I had great self-esteem and felt I was able to do and become anything. It's my belief that every child needs to feel like an emperor a few years in life, to develop a profound trust. But, this wasn't considered a good thing in my family. There were good intentions but my parents were overwhelmed by personal problems and constant emotional neglect was part of my childhood that broke my heart in pieces.

When I was about 8 years old I started to feel unloved, unprotected and that there was something wrong with me. I learned to adjust to fit in. I tried to make everyone happy while we never talked about my parent's emotional instability. That's how I became codependent. I ended up chasing belonging by being who I thought they wanted me to be.

I married my high school sweetheart. He was the first person except my friends that I connected to on a deeper level. But there was an imbalance from the start. I felt I wasn't good enough and though he loved me very much, my discomfort of receiving love and attention led him to feel constantly rejected and I felt guilty. The reluctance and fear to share our true feelings and thoughts led us both to internalize helplessness and shame. We were both so codependent. We started to feel empty and sought happiness from the outer world to hide the pain of an unfulfilled relationship trying to fill the void with different things in life like material possessions that led to economic problems. Nothing was ever good enough. My self worth came from caretaking in the relationship and parenthood and in work.

When I became a mother at the age of 27, I had a lot of knowledge about parenting. I read all the books. Even though I thought I was prepared, I wasn't really prepared at all. Inside I was still a little girl who wanted approval and I thought that by becoming a mother I would finally come to peace and find healing. Everything I lacked as a child I tried to create around me. I really didn't get it. It took time to connect to my first child. The labor ended in a caesarian section and that was a big disappointment and it felt like a personal failure. I wanted to give my child the childhood I did not have, and no mistakes were allowed. I wanted to give him all my love and attention, I wanted his emotions to be accepted and mirrored and I wanted him to have all the material things I did not have. I had made up a picture of a perfect parent, a mother that in reality didn't exist. It was an illusion.

Parenting is all about being yourself, being open; it is about being receptive, about allowing deep emotions, and listening to yourself and to your child. I was feeling vulnerable, swept off my feet really by all negative emotions. You're supposed to be happy right? I felt let down and almost paralyzed by my incapability. Unfortunately, my husband had the same difficulties connecting and left the parenting to me and sadly we couldn't connect at all in this difficult time. We drifted apart and I was feeling guilty for everyone involved and heavily responsible. I didn't know what to do and felt like I was spiraling down into a deep hole.

I decided to bring my son to visit a psychologist at the childcare center. I wanted her and the society to see what an incapable mother I was so that they could make a decision to take my son away from me before I destroyed him completely. This was my firm belief. But strangely the psychologist told me I was the best mother to my son! At first I wanted to have a second opinion because she was obviously out of her mind. While we waited for that second opinion we talked, and she asked if I had heard the story about the two women in the bible who had a dispute about a child and went to Solomon. Solomon turned to God and asked what he should do. And God said: The true mother of the child is the one who couldn't bear to see harm come to her infant. Solomon then suggested they should cut the child in two pieces and give one half to each mother. One of the mothers screamed out to Solomon. *"Please my Lord, give her the living child and do not kill it!"* But the other woman said: *"Neither mine nor yours shall he be. Cut!"* King Solomon said, *"Give her (the mother with compassion) the living child, and do not kill it, for she is his mother!"*

The psychologist made her point with that story and I finally started crying. Then, she gave me homework. I was supposed to gaze into my son's eyes for 5 minutes every day for a week and come back for a second appointment. That week something happened that I will never forget for as long as I live. That week I fell in love with my 4-month-old son. When I gazed into his eyes I felt a subtle warmth inside of my heart; A warmth that became bigger everyday, that melted my heart and grew deeper and deeper love in me for him. I cried and I told him over and over again, "Mama`s here. It's okay honey. I'm never going to let you go. I'm never going to let anything bad happen to you!" Oh the feeling of that! This was the first turning point to find trust, love and happiness. I let the perfect mother "die" to become a loving mother to my son.

It still took a lot of years until I really became aware of my other problems. It took a burnout depression to see the correlation and start to seek interest in personal development. My husband and I started therapy and tried for years and years but sadly we couldn't meet in sympathetic response and didn't reach an understanding. There was only one thing left; the thing we both feared the most.

The winter has come and I've turned into a bird of passage. I left my childhood sweetheart and have endured endless nights of sorrow. Writing it down now, I have tears in my eyes. For half of my life I was lost, giving up parts of myself. Here I am in a new and unknown space. I'm drinking tea in a cafe with my favorite muse, Angela. Her name actually means angel. With her glossy eyes and winter rosy cheeks, she's never been more beautiful, though she shoos it off it's still so. She asks me how it feels to be living on my own. She asks what its like. I tell her it's amazing and difficult at the same time. I feel freedom, lightheartedness and sadness.

Divorce contains a lot of things, several layers; a lot of loss, not just the loss of a partner but loss of my identity and the loss of having the children full-time, the loss of family and friends. Loss of the little things; I miss my garden and fireplace. I miss having a forest just a breathlessly wistful walk away. I miss my daughter's soft little hand in mine, as I follow her to school. I even miss the spiders and the mousetraps with peanut butter we use to have everywhere. I have beloved people in my life, people I miss so much it aches. I miss my sweetheart and the one person who knew me the most. I miss some of my family and friends, including family and friends who seem to think they need to choose sides or who are judgmental about the decision to get divorced. It hurts. I can't help but wonder how people would be responding to me if my husband had died or if I got cancer. I think they`d react another way. But separation and divorce challenges everyone. It creates fear. The opposite of love isn't hate; it is fear! Fear of not being in control. Fear of inner reflection. Fear of changed relationship or friendship. Fear of growing and lack of nurturing.

My new home is nice, small but beautiful and with a lovely energy. I live near my workplace, near culture and city nightlife. There are friendly people everywhere. I have new friends. I feel welcomed in all those little ways of life. The new beginning has slowly clicked into place: My neighbor's friendly welcoming smile, the morning sun glowing on my face when I drink my first coffee on the stairs outside my house. The couple next to me on the bus who are passionately discussing a book they both love. I know what world that book opened in me. The book lays in his lap and her hand beside it, sparkling eyes and laughter, strangely familiar below the surface. I feel warm inside watching them, sitting with my huge paper bags. I feel strong and weak, great and small, lost and found, and all at the same time. Though I'm thinking, I would do it all over again, and again and again. When I share these thoughts it becomes increasingly clear to me. My home address doesn't matter much. I have to follow my heart. The most important things to me are with me. It's ok to hold space for it. Each day is a new day. My heart lightens looking at the horizon. The most important thing is finally right here, inside of me. Amazing that home is so beyond the cliche -its in me, paradise in me, now my heart overflows, because gratitude knows no bounds.

I trust my heart and I am home!

Petra Brynell is a woman, mother and midwife with an innerness that sways like the ocean. She breathes and meets people with great presence from the well inside of her. Petra loves to explore creativity. She loves words because they are close to her soul. A few years ago, she discovered a passion for photography and found a new language to express what's there beyond the obvious. Her dream is to publish a photography book with her own poetry. Petra loves words and would like to read some of yours. Feel welcome to contact her:

petrabrynell@gmail.com
https://instagram.com/_petramidwife_/

Story Five

Awakening a Silenced Motherhood

Carina Halvardsson

I was seventeen years old and found out that I was never going to be able to give birth to any children. In that moment, I was just grateful to be alive. I was almost killed by a mistreatment under a gastrointestinal surgery. That alone can fill a book of disappointments.

I felt raped. I shut down the memories and feelings for thirty-six years and it hurts like hell to get in touch with them again. But I know I have to because the 17-year-old in me is screaming out her frustration, disappointment and anger, of not being seen, listened to and respected as a human being. The doctors got in to my stomach and cut me open. They did not bother to put everything back where it should be. They did not even move my uterus back into the right place when they sewed me together again. They just left me with my pain after destroying my body and the possibility of ever giving birth. I woke up from the anesthesia during surgery and couldn't move or talk. I tried to open my eyes and scream without any success. But I could feel the pain and hear every sound of metal and the rustle of hospital gowns. They were talking about me and I heard the doctor say, "Lucky she isn't fat. It doesn't look good; She is bleeding a lot. Oh my, why is it so hard to put a redhead to sleep? You can't give a person too much anesthetic." Then I passed out. I was between life and death for a few days.

In addition to the pain, it repressed my sexuality by cutting things inside my body. Then no one bothered to talk with me about how it could affect me as I continued to grow into an adult woman. I was left with big scars all over my tummy that still make me want to hide. I feel ugly and shame over it.

Now, I'm rediscovering the seventeen year old me, crying my eyes out and I'm pissed off. I feel so angry that no one was paying any attention to me and what was going on. I just wanted everyone to like me, careful not to be difficult or uncomfortable against authority figures. I was a well-behaved child and wanted my parents to be proud of me.

I am bursting with anger. *Why!!!* (I let my 17-year-old scream out) *How could you just do this to me without explaining anything to me? How did you think I should go on with my life? Where do I put all the sadness, grief and pain? What do you think you taught me by not talking to me about what was happening?*

The silence kept the wound open and unhealed forever. None of the adults, including the physician, spoke to me about the horror I experienced. My parents did not stand up for me against the mistreatment. I followed their lead and was silent.

When I was a teen, I really didn't know who I was. I was bullied almost the whole time I was in school. I tried to please everyone in my vicinity and adapt to the surroundings; that sure didn't help and I hadn't the slightest idea who I was. Because of the operation, I also missed the last time celebration in high school with my friends, a very important milestone in a young persons' life.

I was a worried teen and held a lot of tensions inside my body. Those tensions were about being loved and accepted as I was. Why was I afraid of shouting out LOVE ME!!!! That is all I wanted; To love and be loved.

The grief of not being able to have any children has come and gone during my life. I made a choice to accept the fact that I was not going to change any diapers, dry wretch and blow noses. I knew I wouldn't have a lot of sleepless nights waking up to feed a baby or hold a soft, little life close to my chest and bond while I was breastfeeding. I would never look a baby in the eye and feel the deep connection that is pure bliss or have the ability to experience the spiritual nourishment while it flows between mother and child. I would never look and wonder what traits or features my child had received from me; Never hear the words "this I have learned from my mom."

I wonder how it would be to be some one's grandmother. I know how it was to have one and that was one of the best memories from my childhood. Perhaps the hardest is not being able to share that experience with other women, my own mom. Maybe it's an illusion, but I have a feeling that the bond between mother and daughter when you have your own children is special. It's like a circle is completed in a way.

When I was a little girl I always said that I would have many children of my own. There would be so many that the space of our home would be too little or small. (I would let them grow up in my parents' home.) There would be children everywhere even up on the hat shelf. Hahaha!!! I'm laughing out loud when I think about the wish I had. I know it was my loving heart that wanted to include everyone. I had a dream about everyone on the planet being a huge family. I had a strong feeling that everyone in the world could help each other. When we walked to my grandmother's house on Sundays, I imagined that we could get help using a toilet or having a glass of water from a lady in a house we passed. How convenient that would have been. My wishes in that time were not too big or were they? Maybe it was about serving the whole without selfishness and restrictions. I had a big picture inside my mind but I couldn't express myself back then.

Now I see the biggest issue here: The longing for connection. Even if I didn't have the opportunity to be a mother I carry the wisdom in my DNA. I'm designed to be a mother even if I didn't give birth to a child. It has always been a part of who I am.

The loss of a very good friend helped me to see myself on a deeper level. I am a cancer survivor. She passed away from her cancer last year. I told her that I would tell her story when she was not here anymore. To honor her existence and my own, I will talk about the importance of speaking and being honest with our feelings.

We talked a lot about holding things inside and not speaking out about what we really felt in certain areas. The deep connection between us during her last year and a half of life was amazing. She opened up a special place in my heart and I am forever grateful.

I'm giving birth to an idea of spreading universal love by touching peoples bodies and hearts. I will do that by continuing the philanthropy work together with the organization Vision For All. To help adults and children in poor countries to get glasses for free so they can study and work and provide for themselves and their families. I will continue to voluntarily work with restorative justice programs so that the broken family ties can be repaired. "It is the one who has been hurt that hurts other people." It's so important to me that these damaged relationships are healed. It has to be in a loving, trusting way like a motherhood way ☺ I would love to work with helping girls in the world to feel just as accepted as boys. Without each other, we cannot exist. I want to be the mother of the children of the world. I dedicate myself to these things 100% just like a mother to her children.

I have tried to get in touch with the conclusion of this story and I ask myself, what is underneath? To give is to receive; to receive is to give. I accepted that I would not have children and I also shut down a part of me. I know what I really want is to belong and feel connected to a tribe. That is what my DNA is shouting out. In my whole life I have been struggling with the fact that I couldn't give birth and settled for being disconnected and not belonging. I need to allow myself to be a part of something or someone. I have always waited for my turn or the right moment. But it has never come until now. I am ready to step into the world and take my place. Step in to the world and say, "Here I am finally". It's time to take a big step into the world and show some action. I am not going to waste any more time. For too long, I have hidden and silenced my feelings that struggled to show themselves; The truth has set me free and I'm giving birth to the unborn part of myself.

I am opening up and trusting the loving force in me to handle receiving and giving as a beautiful dance. I will take the opportunity to thank all the people who have been there for me in times of difficulty. Their love for me is unconditional. We need each other to survive and it's great!

My mission in life is to spread Universal Love. I use all of this love inside me and pour it into the children in the world, the love I would have used with the dream from my childhood, a house filled of children and love. I listen and find God's vision for me.

And I continue to give love to my 17-year-old self. I let her be angry, to get it out and then together, we walk hand in hand to spread our Universal Love.

Carina Halvardsson: I am a body therapist, lecturer and a Qi Gong teacher. I give your body unconditional support to release tensions and trauma so your life energy can flow smoothly and vitalize you. I give you tools for relaxation and to silence your mind. I teach you how to use it in an easy way. Everything is about slowing down and making it simple. It's not your mind that needs to feel safe it's your body. I use my voice to inspire you through my lectures. I'm a dedicated visionary and I want to spread universal love. www.carinahalvardsson.se

Part Two

I AM SHIFTING

"I was learning to differentiate between my needs and my wants and this powerful lesson had to be mastered before I could move forward."

~Sarah Ban Breathnach,
Author of Simple Abundance

Story Six

The Freedom Story

Tazima Davis

"A girl should be two things: who and what she wants."
— Coco Chanel

Fire Sprinkler

I knew I could not go home, or live another hour for that matter, without having this conversation. I had gathered all my strength to make this request because my feet felt like two cement blocks as I made my way over to ask him to join me to "chat for a moment". Although it had been a lovely, relatively mild mid-winter night in New York, I needed privacy for these words I was about to share and there was only one warm-ish indoor space available at the venue, which was still bustling with clean up activity after a well-attended event.

We descended the cinder block stairwell together in silence. On a landing between floors, I turned and leaned lightly on the wall for support. There was a searing heat in my belly spreading rapidly to my face and head, though wasn't enough to set off the fire sprinklers. I would have welcomed the relief of cool water sputtering and spewing forth to douse my head and body.

He stood in front of me quietly, patiently. I paused, breathed deeply. I softly studied the red pipe and the fan-shaped deflector as I reluctantly and necessarily began. The words came in a trickle at first, I brought my eyes down to meet his. More words came, but I felt frustrated: even carefully chosen words could only approximate my true thoughts and feelings.

I wanted to run. I wanted to fight. I wanted to yell and scream and cry and rip flesh and burn and break things and kick through doors. I wanted to tear down the walls of this building and the walls between people and the walls that protect fearful tender hearts. What I wanted to communicate most was that I wanted to be met with fresh eyes of curiosity, rather than stereotypically framed conclusions. I did my best and fought to stay present as I consciously, slowly, and deliberately placed each word into this unwieldy and ponderous conversation.

Words

The most difficult kind of conversation is one where the person on the receiving end (the receiver) must reveal that the person on the giving end (the giver) has participated in racist behavior even though the giver wants to be seen as a "good person". This conversation was made more complex since the white man, with whom I was about to speak, was a sexual partner. Our most recent sexual encounter was just a few days prior to the moment that he thought it was ok to use the n-word with me as a term of endearment.

These words he sent to me via text produced shock, disappointment, and a tumultuous churning in my stomach. They hit a deep place in the foundation of my identity as a self-determined free individual. Though I don't fit neatly into any stereotypical box you'd attempt to put me in based on how I look or sound, I considered that perhaps self-determination and individuality is a luxury of the dominant culture. It was disturbing that my sexuality was also subject to stereotypical assumptions.

I do not remember everything I said. I know that I shared my unusual personal context and the dizzying number of perspectives from which I experienced that moment. I told him that it wasn't my responsibility to make him feel comfortable about what happened. Nor was it my duty to individually absolve him of the guilt of the deeds done by people who look like him just because I know him. I asked him to be an ally, to stop using the n-word, and to be vigilant in letting others know that he does not approve of its use. I wanted him to know that I felt violated and that there is nothing light, endearing, or comical about that word.

The violation I felt was not only perpetrated by him individually; I also felt violated by a collection of implications. The most unsettling of which was that my sexuality has political, racial, and class threads running through it. Even in the most private areas of my life, I still deal with the burden of being personally and individually responsible for my group identity. In this situation with this man, I felt exhausted by this burden.

Fortunately, he heard me. Some of his response was fairly typical where he tried to relate his own experience to mine; which, unfortunately, does not show up as empathy but rather as denial, dismissal, deflection. In the rest of the conversation, his words let me know that he was stretching; he was starting to see a new perspective. This is all I wanted. I didn't think we would heal the world in one conversation, but perhaps I could shift one perspective of one human from unconscious violation toward conscious curiosity.

Otherness and Belonging

Before I go any further, I want to put down the burden of responsibility to speak for "my people", whoever you think (or even whoever I think) that may be. My experience is as a foreign-born black woman in America and growing up around all kinds of people. My world already includes a mix of everyone. So "inclusion" and "diversity" aren't my words; they are words of the majority culture stretching to create more space for a non-primary thought. It is impossible to overlook or forget because when I am included, I bring the diversity to the gathering.

I am a threshold dweller, a translator, a go-between, a de-facto diplomat, and to me, cultural and racial homogeneity is "other". I have visited and lived in lots of places. I feel I don't quite "belong" anywhere and I have never ever "fit in". Fortunately, I've learned lots of "languages" (or communication codes) along the way in order to connect with whoever I'm with wherever I am. In this country, where I am a member of an "other" or "minority" culture, I am nearly always being reminded of my surface-level differences and I rarely feel seen for my similarities or my individual uniqueness.

I also want to let you know that I don't want to talk about freedom and identity and sexuality/sensuality. I didn't choose it. I never set any aspirations for being some kind of freedom fighter or an orator for liberation. Quite frankly, I'd rather be watching dystopian future-based science fiction movies or discussing the benefits of low-end torque of my favorite Italian motorcycles.

I don't think any of the leaders of movements ever planned on being the face of change. They just believed in something strongly, like I do, and started sharing their vision and discussing their ideas. Perhaps my assignment is to discuss my own freedom because my interests and life circumstances have lined up in such a way that I'm often straddling communities, traversing circles, connecting networks, and I have found an inherent freedom in the act of going between.

Socio-Sexual Politics

As a member of a "racial minority" group, there is this unspoken race responsibility: that we have to make sure that we look good and behave well so as not to confirm any negative stereotypes. This directly influences the way I dress, speak, and act, always, with no days off. In my sexuality, although I seek freedom of expression, I find it sometimes challenging to balance other people's expectations of my sex life based on my race. In a way, I become responsible for all the past and future interactions that this person of the majority culture has had or may have.

The more active I became in sex positive circles, the more I felt I had to assert my standards of what is permissible as a term of endearment. While many of the white women embraced the terms "slut" and "bitch", I declined participation. There is already an expectation that black women are angry and therefore are bitches, and not in the good way. And there is often a disdainful expectation that black women are more sexual and therefore inherently sluttier.

As a sex, intimacy, and relationship coach for women, I often encourage women to directly state and cleanly request the sex and relationships they want. Yet, ironically, there are ways that I curtail my activities, or at least the discussion of my activities, to manage the expectations of those around me. Not to mention, the curvier shapes of my black body make clothes look different and whisper to the imagination about my specific and the general sexual prowess of black women.

Freedom as Experience

My search for the truth of my being, my path of personal growth, has largely been a process of going down and in. There have been bountiful blessings and the tricky part is for me to remember to feed my soul with the gratitude for them. The strength and power I have cultivated from the bumps on the road (and from the difficult conversations with travel mates) are clear and felt when I connect with people personally or professionally. It is important for me to distinguish that freedom is not a destination or somewhere to get to.

Along the way, I learn more about every aspect of my true self. Layer by tender layer is peeled back, removed, or burned away to reveal more and more of the truth that wants to be expressed. These parts of my one united self, touch every area of my life and any attempts to dissect out any inconvenient or unlovable part is a recipe for inner turmoil. My job is to learn of them, love them, and integrate them whether they are spiritual, sexual, personal, interpersonal, bold, or scared.

The more I pursue this experience of freedom for myself, the more of an example I become, and the more people around me feel the strength to do the same for themselves. I am constantly identifying mental shackles of my own and in conversation, I tell my story to reveal places where others haven't realized theirs. As I traverse these circles as a de-facto diplomat, I am teaching people along my path and offering small gifts of freedom.

I have a deep desire to be seen for my individuality. I want to experience freedom without the binds of social expectations. I want to feel the luxury of self-determination and be truly "seen" by those with whom I interact. My wish for the world is this: that we work together to tear down the walls that keep people from using innocent child-like curiosity to see all the unique gorgeousness of every single other human. I want that for myself and for everyone else.

Tazima Davis is a national speaker, author, and coach. She helps professional women attract the right partner and have better communication around sex and relationships. Over the past 5 years, Tazima has coached and taught about sex and relationships in cities nationwide including San Francisco, Los Angeles, Chicago, Washington DC, and New York City. Her experience also includes 6 years as a food scientist, 8 years as a holistic health and life coach, and 9 years as a yoga teacher. In her free time, Tazima loves geeking out about anything related to motorcycles, science fiction, or the physics of consciousness. http://www.InfiniteRelating.com tazima.davis@gmail.com

Story Seven

Tangle

Karen A. Porter

Bleah.

Fuck the onion. Layer after layer after layer. Enough is enough. I am tired of not being okay with who I am exactly now, in this minute, but I have no idea what else to do. What I have done is not enough. Never enough. It mirrors how I feel about myself. Not enough. Fat, lazy, stupid.

I have been writing every day and I still have less than 600 words for this story. This is not a comfortable place. I continue the process of examining, tolerating the discomfort of the emotions surfacing and not knowing the exact moves to make.

Go to the broken place.

Years of therapy and support, I constructed a life, started a business, began a relationship that has become a thirty year marriage.

Still devoid of trust, I continue protecting myself from destruction. I built a facade. Strong, self sufficient, confident, efficient, not caring about the opinions of others. This surface layer covered the jumbled mess of how I internalized what happened.

The beginning is not the abuse. It is deeper, more primal.

Each step of therapy, workshops, teachers and books led to insight and understanding and many times a momentary sense of healing. But now, it feels like the wound kept being bandaged. I applied different ointments, tried different treatments to make the mess disappear.

I hate the onion metaphor. Healing one thing, learning a lesson only leading to the next and the next and the next, layers of the onion.

At my core, I want to be different. My family is good *even though I feel I am not loved for being me. I have to censor myself for approval and acceptance.* I like my life.

I just don't like me.

The snow is falling. I am writing again. More words, painful words. Being with them and the feelings. I understand the compulsion to cut, to feel something, anything but what I am feeling. As I remember, I write. Eating for sustenance, not to numb. Being with these feelings differently.

I ache. I am sore and sad. I feel broken and defeated. I learned to detach from feelings at a very young age. Barely older than a toddler, self-preservation was primary. Feelings bad. Turn off to survive. Devoid of sensation, I navigated through a childhood of sexual abuse and teenaged years of denial.

My life story is a jumbled up mess of knots.

From my father, I learned the mastery of untying knots. I find the process meditative. While others say they would just cut out the mess, I examine, retrace paths and slowly solve the riddle of the overs, unders and arounds of a tangled up mess.

For the most part, I had a privileged, idyllic childhood. And I was sexually abused. I had parents who loved me and cared for me, doing the best they could. Still, I was not protected from a predator. I felt unloved while I was loved. I was cared for and abandoned. I was used, betrayed and abused. It all coexisted. The melange of feelings and judgments continue to coexist. I am allowing myself to feel the mix and mess and confusion of what I constructed as a child and carried inside, buried deep for over fifty years.

As an avid knitter, finding some great wool at yard sales and thrift stores, I am no stranger to knots. Even though each tangle is unique and there is no one manual or map to follow to undo a mass of interwoven knots, there is a general process to untangling.

I look at the overall mass and determine the beginning and the end, finding the thread that leads up to the mess and where the yarn emerges. I look for clues of pathways.

At nineteen, a car accident stopped my attending college. My life stopped. I cracked open, exposing the long buried pain and memories of terror, lies, control, torture and rape.

Usually there will be some easy undoing in the beginning. Sometimes the friction of the knotting and the undoing process can cause the wool to felt together where the outermost fibers will interlock to form a connection that will need to be separated to restore the integrity of the single thread. As I get closer to the center, the twisting and turning is tighter and it is more difficult to see the next steps.

I accept the existence of the mess inside. When I allow myself to feel the pain of worthlessness at my core, I cry. I want to be happy. I want to feel awesome. I pretend. How do I banish the hole, fill the emptiness?

Nothing can rework the past. What is done is done. How can I salvage my life?

A tug on the yarn can reveal a pathway, but when it makes the knot tighter, surrounding threads can be eased, loosened to make room for threading through the end. At the very center, the knot will be the tightest and the yarn will be the most stressed.

For several nights I have slept well. Solid, sound sleep with some crazy but inconsequential dreams. A shift, a welcome change from a long stretch of restless and interrupted sleep and disturbing dreams.

Even when the yarn shows wear or damage, it can be used or spliced to strengthen it and become part of the fabric as each stitch builds on the one before it.

The theory of breakthrough and insight coming in moments of relaxation. The shower is my place of connection. After weeks of steeping in the discomfort of my feelings, clarity came in the shower. The beginning of understanding. Not fully formed but a glimpse of the work that lies ahead, a possible pathway.

No knot is ever so tight it cannot be untied given gentle movements and patience, analysis and intuition. The only decision to be made is to commit to the process of untangling.

I desired love, approval and to be cherished for me. A gaping ache, an empty place of need and longing. There as a baby, a toddler, a young girl. With two family businesses, work came first. My father's mother owned a bathing beach. She made a year's money between Memorial Day and Labor Day. The summer I was born, my mother worked on the 4th of July. I was born on the 8th.

I had a summer babysitter the first couple years of my life. Then I spent summers with my mother's parents. I remember my parents visiting once a week for dinner. My grandfather grew most of their food. Mom Mom tended the garden, canning and preserving food for the winter in addition to the normal cooking, laundry, cleaning and church and social obligations.

My aunt and her husband lived next door. Bob worked the swing shift at the GM plant. Home during the morning and afternoons, the busy time for Mom Mom, available to give lots of attention to a needy little girl. The grooming period of pedophilia is all about attention, bonding and building trust. Little by little, the trust is betrayed. The inappropriate behavior is introduced slowly, incrementally, while the attention continues.

My younger brother was born the summer I was five. By then, two uncles were abusing me. The younger uncle, learning French in high school taught me how old I was in French. "Sank! Sank! Sank!" I declared as he masturbated me and himself.

At six, more pain with the enforced separation of having to start school. Compliance and unquestioning obedience does not feed the need for validation and acknowledgment of unique gifts. With my brother still a baby, my mother was happy I spent weekends with her parents.

Then I was seven and Bob fucked up big time, getting caught in an affair with a barmaid. His inappropriate behavior with my older sister came to light. Emily was eight years old when I was born. When Bob touched her, she told. Mom Mom had dealt with it by telling Bob never to do such a thing again.

"Good girls don't tell." A mantra repeated to me and repeated by me. Bob had learned to be more cautious, starting earlier and more slowly with me. My outraged father scared me when he demanded to know if Bob had ever 'hurt' me. "No." What he did never hurt. I did not know what he was asking. Because I did not understand, Bob got away with it.

Emboldened, the abuse escalated. He knew he could do anything. He had successfully trained his victim. I was trapped. I had no choice. It was my fault. I wanted the good attention. I had said nothing. I didn't know. I didn't understand. I was stupid. I was dirty. I was worthless. There was nothing I could do. I was powerless, resigned to my fate, both physical and spiritual.

Seven is the age of reason, said the nuns. There was no awareness of predators, adult responsibility or the vulnerability of children. We were responsible for the choices we made and the sins we committed. By seven, the die was cast. I was dirty, sinful, shame-filled and culpable.

To survive, I learned to not feel. Pressure, weight, huffing and puffing. Objects, fingers, an elbow by my face, a chest moving above me. Feeling so small. Used. Hopeless.

Live a lie. Hide a secret. See me and you see my shame. No one can know. So afraid of being found out. Judgment. So needy I would respond to *any attention, so stupid to not have adult insight as a child. I am disgusted and feel disgusting. I deserve nothing.*

In my child-mind I think it was my fault. My adult mind knows that my family put work before everything. The signs I showed, the symptoms I had were mysteries. A pediatrician who was more concerned with my weight than the underlying reason. The very qualities that made me a creative, self contented, attention seeking child, made me the perfect target for a child-fucker.

Rebellion, attitude, outrage over what had been. Seeing how it came to be. Recognizing the weaving of action and reaction, teachings and misunderstandings. I see that at my core I have turned all my anger and hatred onto myself. I would never think of saying to others anything close to what I tell myself. I would not tolerate anyone saying what I tell myself. So critical, blaming, focused on faults and flaws.

I have desire and I feel undeserving. Both are true. To more fully feel the desire, I am feeling all that is there. By feeling all that is there, I am loosening the spaces to allow for new feelings. I have yearning and pain. I am feeling compassion for the unprotected me. I am starting to turn some emotions onto their true and deserving targets.

I am in the mix, the mess, the tangle. I am co-existing with discomfort and getting comfortable with not knowing the formula or all the steps on this path to peace with all that lies inside. I am glimpsing at a way to begin to forgive myself for being innocent, a child caught in a web. It feels like the "I" and "me", of "then and now" can untangle. I can begin to appreciate the uniqueness of me and recognize my strength, learning to cherish and love while calming the judge and critic.

I don't have it all sorted out, yet I know it is possible to start feeling whole and happy and deserving and perfect right now in this minute. I commit to continuing this process. By seeing more and feeling deeper, I am closer to sorting it out. The knots are many and tight and I have all the patience and skill I need.

Karen A Porter is the author of the Live Your Life With Attitude Workbook/Journal, available on Amazon in print and e-book version. Currently on the Advisory Board of the non-profit organization Heal My Voice, Karen is a contributing author to all the US HMV books. www.mamaporter.com https://www.facebook.com/MamaPorterAttitude

Story Eight

Unfolding the gift from God

Marie Ek Lipanovska

I was one day from death when I realized I hadn't yet fully lived as me. I decided I would make one last effort or God would never forgive me. But to find the strength to once again rise out of nothing, I knew I had to accept all of my desires once and for all, and then find a way to connect to them. I needed to let go of the excuses, all of which came from one scary thought. "They will abandon me and I will not be allowed to belong if I am all of me." I looked at myself in the mirror and knew I couldn't abandon that woman before me one more time. She looked at me with imploring eyes and whispered. "My desires are God, sensuality, and money. Please don't judge me and my desires anymore."

I am a co-creator by nature and I manifest through my desires. I know that for a fact. I grew up in the vibration and environment of lack on so many levels and layers. Lack of faith. Lack of love from a father. Lack of money and financial freedom. Lack of ambition. Lack of role models for how to embody sexuality, sensuality, feminine grace, or elegance. Lack of healthy love relationships. We never spoke about spirituality, burning desires and the purpose of life.

I was raised in survival mode. A good life meant having a job, paying the bills, and not becoming an alcoholic. That vision was not enough for me. It was not the life I wanted for myself. I came in contact with my deeper desires when my sexuality awakened as a teenager. I had big dreams. I wanted to change the world. Be rich. Be famous. Make an impact. Do something meaningful. Leave a legacy.

I could easily imagine myself in the future. So I decided that by the time I was 30 years old I would be married to a kind man, have children, live in a house, own a car, and have savings in the bank. More than anything I wanted a loving, present father for my children. So I got what I asked for. In my marriage I stepped fully into motherhood and we co-created wealth, comfort, and a great family.

But something crucial was missing. I was totally disconnected from my other desires and I never let my husband fully into my heart and soul. A couple of years after my 30th birthday I began to feel stuck. My soul was slowly dying. I didn't understand what was wrong until I one day realized I had no intentions for life, no goals to focus on, and I hadn't acknowledged my sexual desires and the longing for a deeper physical and spiritual connection. I had pushed those emotions away for so long and covered them up in a lot of shame and guilt. I felt unworthy and undervalued. I hated sex, while inside, I was screaming for love and attention. I gained a lot of weight and got depressed.

I was 37 when I went away on a retreat. Not as a participant, but as a journalist, writing an article about spirituality. I joined in the retreat activities so that I could share my personal experience. That was what they wanted from me at the magazine. We did a "vision cloud" exercise at the retreat. It connected me back to my imagination and my desires. Even though I was there as a professional writer, I couldn't neglect my personal emotions any longer. In the vision cloud I wrote, "living in a new home, having a love relationship, being a professional coach, and running my own business. Deadline: before I turn 40 years old." One month before that birthday, against all odds, I had manifested everything. It was pure divine magic and timing.

When the love relationship arrived, I found out that God and sexuality came hand in hand for me. They were interdependent. When my soul opened up, my body followed. Sexual connection became a highway to a heavenly connection with God. In this new relationship, I often cried silently after climax. Each time, something in me broke open and there were no longer any walls to keep up, no fears to hold on to, nor masks to hide behind. In that place of surrender I felt so relaxed and at peace with everything. It was as if I was being held in the hands of God. Absorbed by love. No thoughts. Just pure presence. No separation. Just connection. I loved being me when we were lying in bed and the sun was shining through the window. I could hear the birds sing outside and our bodies were covered only in a couple of white sheets. We would stay in bed and sleep for a while. Then wake up again and just enjoy being connected in the stillness and silence. I remember we both loved that softness in me that came after we had had sex. My mouth was closed. My fingers gently followed his eyebrows, his nose, around his mouth and through his hair. My kisses were soft and I placed my head on his chest so that I could listen to his heart. In those quite moments after lovemaking I felt my own feminine sensuality; A side of me I wasn't connected to in my daily life. I wanted more of that tender presence and pure pleasure.

I loved my coaching business, my new home and the man in my life, all of which I had listed as my desires. But what I forgot to write in my vision cloud was money. I had lost my longing for financial safety and freedom. I only knew about manifesting out of lack. When I entered my new love relationship and started my own business, I had money. My desire was to invest the money and my experience in humanity, God, and love. So I did. But as a couple, we were unable to co-create financial wealth and hold that material energy, so I lost the foundation of comfort and security that took me 17 years to build. My burning desires had the ability to create prosperity, but I couldn't maintain it because, underneath it all, I had manifested out of lack.

During four years I healed the many layers and levels of lack that I carried with me since childhood. I did that within Heal My Voice as a participant and as a leader. Towards the end of that period, my body went into starvation mode, and I was slowly dying, and barely surviving. I had lost almost everything including my old identity. It was a process of "letting go and letting God" and it continued until all that remained of me was the deep awareness of "I am." When I was one day from suicide, God, with His grace, stepped in and told me the truth about me. Finally, I saw myself through His eyes of unconditional love. I am Eva Marie; daughter of God, mother of three wonderful children and a beloved woman with a deep desire to live in harmony with all that I am and all there is.

One day I sat down in front of my big golden mirror and looked deeply into my own image. I saw a pair of brown eyes filled with so much pure love and compassion. I witnessed a brave heart so devoted to serve God that I could give up my life if that was what He wanted. My eyes were deeper than any ocean. I felt the vibration and the power in my feminine attraction. I finally understood the significance of Her, the woman in me. Gently, I asked myself what She truly wants and desires. At first, She felt fragile and scared. Like a wild animal terrified of being hunted down and afraid of being stripped of Her sensual beauty and sensitivity. Over and over again I connected to Her, me, the woman in the mirror. I spent hours just looking at myself, sensing my vibration and embracing the fullness of my desires. Slowly and gently we melted together, and we remain in that process every day.

My heart tells me I am here to experience a graceful living. That is the core of being me. Graceful living is the essence of my lifestyle when all my desires align, and all my feminine aspects, the daughter, mother, and woman are one. Deep down inside, I know that feeling of graceful living where I am the red rose petals resting on top of the white sheets. God is that bed linen. Life is that mattress. The man is the bed frame. I can hear the birds singing outside the slightly open bedroom window. It is a place of total surrender to God and to life. There is nothing more to let go of. This is the core of my interdependency, knowing that I am not enough for myself. I cannot be everything on my own. Here I am free to co-create and be held by the love of a man. I trust him to be the bud holding us and connecting us to the divine stem so that I can blossom and be the fragile petals on our rose. A love grounded in faith and truth.

I have learned both humility and gratitude. I experienced God's grace and mercy when I was down on my knees and asking to be rescued from death. I am opening up that divine gift now, very carefully allowing His love and grace to unfold into a graceful life. I trust God's divine timing and that I will have all that I need. I have reconnected to the protective mother in me and her desire for money. I know that financial freedom creates comfort and security for me and my children. Money brings us opportunities to enjoy the richness and beauty of life. With money we can choose where to live, what to eat, and we can invest in whatever we are passionate about. I am no longer willing to struggle trying to manifest on my own. I am handmade by God and He knows what I need much more than I do. I have decided to rest in my feminine longing to belong to a man, life, and God. I trust my own receptivity and elegance. I am free to embrace the fact that I am never enough. I need so much from God, life, and those around me to feel fulfilled and alive. I am not here to be everything. I am here to be me. That is the life I was given, and for that I am deeply grateful.

*"I am **Marie Ek Lipanovska**, a Swedish publisher of Women's Voices. Through global book programs I teach feminine leadership, and the mastery of listening and speaking from an open heart. On my podcast I invite women from all countries to share their wisdom and life experiences. I am the founder of Heal My Voice Sweden and an author of sensual short stories. My foundation is my Christian faith and my courage comes out of the love for my three children. I am known for my presence of essence. More than anything I am romantically in love with life."*

www.healmyvoicesweden.com

Story Nine

Conversations with My Body:
Shifting from Shame into Self-Acceptance and Love

Shawn Catherine Fisher
(aka Safira)

You know those conversations we have within ourselves -- the scary ones, the angry ones, the "I would never judge you, but I'm judging you" ones? I have had them a lot in my life. I'm happier now, more in-touch with my emotions, my body, my purpose and place in this world. While the conversations still exist, they are much fewer and farther in-between "sessions".

Since being diagnosed with HSV 2 – genital herpes – in late 2013, much has changed. I have gone from having knocked-down, dragged-out fights inside and with my body to someone who can stand in raw vulnerability, loving my body in a way I never dreamed would exist. I am thankful to mentors, family and friends for helping me with this journey. Yet, most of all, I am filled with gratitude that I listened to everything my body told me along the way – especially those dark spots that needed to have the light shined on them.

I want this to be a gentle story – especially for those with any form of "shadows" with which they are presently "sitting". Please know that this is my journey; and I am speaking from a place of "I". While there may be areas that bring intense emotion to you, I live with herpes every day. What I have realized is that getting herpes is one of the best things that ever happened to me – and I will tell you why.

I will not tell you how I got herpes. I feel as if others have shared their experiences in that arena much better than I could do. I *will* say that I did not go shopping for an STI (Sexually Transmitted Infection) with the check-out coupon **GIFTFORLIFE**, or hoping to get a tattoo of my body's newly developed hashtag: **#notakebacks**.

When I received the news, I was shell-shocked; but not because of the diagnosis. I was deeply and negatively affected by the callous care shown to me by trusted medical professionals. Plus, I was floored by my own mind – how I reacted to hearing the word "herpes". How could I, of all people, be having such horrible thoughts about myself? I am a strong and vocal sex positive advocate. I live my life from a place of no shame as well as "sex is 'feel good', not 'feel guilty'" mindset. I promote "safe is sexy" – always with an emphasis on self-respect, knowledgeable consent, responsibility and accountability. And herpes "happened" to me??? I was mortified. Yet, my humiliation was not that I had this STI. It was that I had made the choice to trust someone and that trust was violated.

I immediately was thrown into a dark tailspin of thoughts, some of which were: "I'll never have sex again; I hate my body; I am stupid for being fooled; I want to destroy the person that did this to me" – and the *biggest ones* – "I'm unclean; I'm impure; I'm disgusting; I want to die." As someone who lives with PTSD (Post Traumatic Stress Disorder) and hypomania, these feelings did not bode well. I fell into a rabbit hole of my own devising – burrowed within my haunted, troubling, horrible mind.

The demand to protect myself was paramount: true self-care, connection to me and others, being present and engaged. All of that was gone. I did what I always have done – I shielded myself in invulnerability. But it was a false door into my own self-created hell. What I now realize is that even when I felt I had passed from the "Valley of the Shadows" again into the light, my hypomania was in full force. The armor with which I shielded myself ultimately moved into full self-destruction. This period lasted nearly one year. I had alternate stages of complete isolation to "putting myself out there" dating, but never having sex; to hating to touch and be in-touch with my body; to going to social events; but never engaging, Finally, there was the over-inflated self awareness" where I only allowed my humorous, very confident persona to show up.

Lack of accountability and responsibility for my medical needs landed me in the hospital on two separate occasions, both of which were life-threatening. My body was rusting and rotting, desperately trying to throw-out all of its poison; but my pride could not allow that. So, I fought to keep everything inside – anything I thought "you" could use to hurt me in any way and I absorbed it back into my body system. In the process, I was committing slow suicide.

The past eighteen months since my herpes diagnosis have been some of the hardest times of my life. It also has been the most rewarding because I confronted what I feared the most in my life – and lived to tell it. Taking accountability and responsibility for my own gainful story has helped me recognize where shame kept me hiding in invulnerability.

Here is the truth: it was not the herpes' diagnosis that was doing this "to" me. It was my abject fear that I could have no more pretenses in any relationship I wanted to develop. I had to be direct, honest, communicate more. Finally, after over fifty years on this planet, I needed to face facts: stringently negotiating and attempting to control every square on my cleverly built chessboard was not the same as mindfully, fully living. The thought left me scared to my core and bone-weary. What was worse, what left me in a dreadful, cold sweat? I was honest, if only with myself, and knew I needed help; I never would be able to move forward on my own. I hated that truth most days more than I loved myself enough to fight to live.

I recognized past hurts, resentments and anger. I forgave and asked forgiveness (a daily practice) – and let the past finally take a well deserved rest. I stopped fearing my own success, embracing "failure" as a part of that process. I learned to love openly, fully, mindfully, fiercely and peacefully. My vulnerability, which I always shunned, is beautiful and soul-searing.

I appreciate and am aware when and if shame still occurs in my life. Now I know and recognize it is my choice to lovingly move forward in its lessons and through it into deeper connection, power and success. By being present in all of my moments I connect to each breath of possibility. And that feels magnificent.

DISPOSABLE

shell shocked
bell broken
light dimmed
dark shadowed minds filled with craven whim
of those whom believed and partook of me in
sin
and reveled in it all the more

i chased my valueless self into a non-living
Hell
day after enduring day
while my mind reeled through its spinning
wheel
to hold onto my fractured humanity through
its insanity

no one wept

invulnerability hid me
from a world in which I wanted to be seen
but could not afford the luxury of exposure
to whatever elements might steal my
weakened soul
break more of my unloved whole
than I was willing to bare

kept in chains, self-possessed

i parceled pieces of my body's tokens

until at last i realized
i was deciding to remain unwoken
to the good waiting to be shared

yet when i stepped into my power
it was to be devoured
by a world wanting to disconnectedly connect
to kill, to shame, to reduce in flames
to forget its history of being comprehensibly
abject

or worse, still apathetic
to all of the surrounding hate
willingly ignorant to allow love in a new place
not fear-based

a choice -- mine, alone
scarred and beaten, bending, weeping
to shout

i SEE with eyes UNblind
that love is a rainbow of ALL humankind
and i will not sabotage or cast out
anyone from my heart
i love all, for everyone is worthy -- myself,
most of all

for we are our own created
Divine art
living proof that each day is a new start

and WE are not disposable

I AM not disposable

©Safira / January 2015

Shawn Catherine Fisher (aka, Safira) is a human rights activist, artist and author, collaboratively working with global, national and local organizations. Shawn currently is taking courses towards her Masters in Divinity, and feels fortunate to have been exposed to numerous spiritual modalities throughout her life. Shawn chooses to unconditionally love everyone, and believes that through all of her choices this includes joyfully loving and honoring herself and her body.

With her latest Heal My Voice® offering, Shawn's desire is to bring hope to others working through shame into self-love and self-acceptance. She can be found on Instagram and Twitter as @PeacefulSafira.

Story Ten

The raw Truth

Kristina Lovén

I am here to let life love me without apology until I crack wide open. I am here to let her challenge me, pull me to the edge of evolution, kiss my cheeks, caress my neck, dance with me, seduce me, make love to me until I let go into the unknown and all that is left is the sensation of the raw beauty that creates life itself.

It seems like most of the human beings walking on this amazing earth are carrying around a story inside of them. The past. For many years, I walked with my story, breathed my story and acted from the wound of my story; like I was my story. I didn't know that I had another choice. I didn't know that I was so filled up with shame and I was playing small; when I did everything to hide and not stand out from the crowd. I didn't know where the shame came from and I didn't know that it was a collective shame and at the same time a very personal shame and that it still didn't belong to me at all; like it doesn't belong to those billions of women and girls who are daily exposed for abuse, rape and therefore exposed for conscious and unconscious ways of attempting to destroy and shut down the personal power within.

From my childhood, there is a story about the little girl in me that had a growing void inside her chest that somehow gave her asthma, anxiety, and a longing to fill that void up no matter what. And I did. I adopted a truth about myself that I was not worthy. At the age of twelve, I wrote an unseen contract with myself that I was not worth the good and easy path in life. I was just not worth it. I felt so connected to the darkness and destruction and I convinced myself that that must be the path where I could find the safety and the belonging to escape from myself. Living in this body was more than I could cope with. I found it hard to walk on this earth. The little girl longed to come home, to return home. I didn't know that home could be in the sweetness of my own body.

In my early teens, I started to smoke and drink and I couldn't concentrate at all on school. Smoking and drinking wasn't enough so I started to try drugs instead. I developed this pattern of falling in love with the guy that wasn't available and after awhile, if he became interested in me, I thought he was the creepiest guy I could think of. I was longing so much for connection but couldn't bear to let anyone in. I couldn't let anyone like me or feel attracted to me. When I was sixteen, I really wanted to lose my virginity so I gave myself to a guy who was a bit older than me to just get it done. I met some guys after that with a very closed, mistrusting and contracted body.

At the age of eighteen, I quit the job I had in a restaurant. I had tried a lot of drugs, partying with friends but the destructive pattern pulling me down was calling louder and louder. Pulled me Down.

I remember the first time I met him. I was lucky to be invited to his home together with a friend. When I sat on his sofa I melted into his brown eyes and remember the feeling of wanting to save him along with a tickling feeling in my young heart. I felt that I was at home. Here I can stay. And I did stay for 4 years. He didn't offer me heroin but I wanted it. I wanted to try. The wounded part of me wanted to die. I couldn't stand the feeling of pain in my body. So for a couple of years I was deep inside an addiction. This life was filled with men and me; dirty men, stinky men, sleepy men, criminals but all somehow kind to me as the girlfriend of a drug dealer.

And there was chaos. I remember the first time he hit me. I felt so humiliated. I remember when he later hit me with a hammer, pulled my hair so very hard, when he put a loaded gun to my head, when he threatened to kill my little brother if I left him. I remember when he beat me with a hard, wooden clog and then had sex with me. I remember when he threw a knife at me and the tendon in my little finger was broken. I remember when a friend of his gave me money for a taxi and said leave now before he kills you. I left for a couple of hours and then I was back again. Didn't know where to go. No friends left and talking to my parents was the last thing to do.

At the end of this chaotic period, I met another man. He felt like a friend. We were attracted to each other. We had sex a couple of times. He got obsessed with me. I broke up with him and one day when he knocked at my door and I let him in to my home, he raped me. He squeezed the last drops from an already frayed washcloth. I was now around 21 years old. Became a woman in chaos. Somewhere along the way I heard a crystal-clear voice in my head that said: *There must be something more.* It came to a point where I had it. The void that I had filled with drugs now got so big that death was the only way out. Or life. I had lost a lot of weight, was very skinny, I had tried to take an overdose, but the drugs were diluted and not strong enough to kill me. There was a turning point when he told me if I went to sleep he would take his own life. I fell asleep. I woke up and there he was hanging from the ceiling. Now I had the choice to get rid of him, to be free, to let him die. I let him live. And finally I left him. **I** used my strong willpower to end the addiction and had a couple of sessions with a treatment person where the strategy to cope with addiction was to set up goals, not to heal. So I did.

I committed to become a person who would fit in. I started to train my body, learned to eat properly, and got a job. Learned to pay bills. Take responsibility. And I did everything to cover up the deep shame and unworthiness that I had felt since I was a child. Connecting with new girlfriends was a huge thing for me. Breaking years of isolation from a world that was so dark and destructive was challenging.

The next ten years I somehow lived a good life. Met a very kind and loving man, gave birth to two of my lovely children, had some fun, had nice friends and a good social company, caught up on my studies and ended up with several years at the university. But I ignored the calling from my body and soul to heal the little child, the teenager and the young woman in me. I ignored her calling so much until my body was screaming in unbearable pain in my neck and my back. I ignored her calling so much that she sent me a man that brought up the erotically closed down parts in me to the surface in just one evening and that wakeup call took me on a new direction in life.

The new direction brought me to a journey of unfolding layer after layer. Embracing and healing the wounds of my inner child, my teenager and the young woman in me. Slowly letting go of attachments to my life story. Acknowledging the vulnerability it has brought into my life along with the deepest power and strength. I devoted myself to bring me to the other side. To walk through the dark nights with a love warrior's courage and a commitment to face the truth no matter what. I dove into feminine practice. I reconnected with my femininity and the beauty of my body and a deep, never-ending, expanding sisterhood. I slowly landed into my body. A weave of amazing and deeply loving sisters wrapped around me. I bathed and am still bathing in the beauty of devoted and vibrating shaktis from all over the world. I finally found a new truth about myself. The raw truth of being loved beyond the beyond by life itself and being worthy into the core of my purest soul.

A couple of years ago I felt the calling to go into sexual celibacy. I had a longing to reconnect to the sacredness in the sexuality without knowing what that meant. I felt the deep longing to reconnect to the most sacred place in my body. My yoni. I felt the pull to collect the yarns of every sexual meeting I have ever had, good or bad, and let them drop through my body down to the earth where they all were transformed to nourishment. I had the willingness to face the path I had chosen and to take full responsibility whatever that meant. These two years of purification left me with a feeling of a golden shimmering innocence.

It was summertime and I felt ready to leave the celibacy and walk into life with a childlike curiosity and a lust to explore life and my sexuality in a new way. I met a beautiful man a couple of times. And for the first time ever I felt whole after a sexual meeting. I got more curious, was it only with this man I could feel whole? Was it because he was so gentle, present and empathic?

Recently another beautiful, tenderhearted man crossed my path. He gives me the invaluable gift of challenging me to be received fully. Just as I am. He helps me to break through my limiting pleasure roof and he is uncompromising in a way that makes me surrender deep into my erotically and pouring femininity. In his presence my body relaxes deeply, opens up and melts.

The feminine power is so strong that it acts in the name of love, care and justice in the benefit of the highest good for all living beings. The feminine power is a love warrior that aches her pure heart during dark times while protecting the earth´s children with her love.

Suddenly the moment is here. I receive life. I open my mouth and drink the nectar. Let it drip slowly, almost like thick honey. I feel the taste of it. Love the smell. I let the nectar renew my cells in my body. Feeling the life enter my body and opens up my inner universum. My inner yoniversum. That longing that has been with me for several years is now inside my body, settles down in my womb, the most beautiful sacred space for creation. That longing has been my direction, my most challenging friend and my guide into deep trust and faith. That longing that has required a lot of courage, a deep willingness and even more trust now shows up as the deepest relaxation my body has ever experienced. A moment of bliss. A moment of connection. A moment of being seen and a deep trust in another human being. A deep trust in myself. A deep trust in Life.

Kristina Lovén *A passionate and devoted lover of life. Project assistant and apprentice during the HMV project Sensual Voices. Co-writer to the Swedish books Värdefulla Röster (Worthy Voices) and Frigörande Röster (Liberated Voices). She lives in Sweden with her beloved family.*
kristina_loven@yahoo.se

Photography: http://www.idaninasofia.com/

Part Three

I AM Surrender

"When resistance is gone, the demons are gone."

~Pema Chödrön

Story Eleven

Time to Stop Hiding

Lisbeth **Jönsson**

A crack in the illusion

I stand outside a window looking in. I see a
fireplace with sparkling flames warming the
surroundings. I see a set table with the best
china waiting for guests. I see a Christmas
stocking loaded with gifts. I see the Christmas
tree decorated with beautiful glitter, lights and
ornaments. I see the perfect family looking
lovingly at each other wishing the best. When I
look deeper in the picture I see the food
nobody has eaten. I see the spoiled dreams of

the family. I see the running mascara on a cheek. I see the crack in the illusion and the reality gets under my skin. It gets cold; the fire is out, dishes in a pile in the kitchen. Silence. No one speaks about it. I hear sobbing from a child's bed. The joyful time of the year has once again turned into pain, worry and sadness. It was not Father Xmas who came for a visit this year but Uncle Alcohol. He left a disgusting smell of aftershave with no mercy on his way ahead.

A New Flat

Today I received the keys to my new flat, a place of my own. Last year I bought a wall decoration with the words *"Deep rest for the soul."* I didn't know why I bought it back then, just that I felt a strong hunch to do it. The words on the decoration were in my mind when I was looking for a new place to stay. That was the energy that I was looking for. I also had written four core words on a little piece of paper: *Love, Joy, Truth and Simplicity*; Words that would lead me now that I was about to leave my love relationship after 16 years, a relationship that has been visited by Uncle Alcohol for several years.

Earlier today, before I went to the real estate agent, I packed a few things that had special meaning to me to bring to the flat. The wall decoration was obvious, so was the piece of paper with the four words, a pot with a green plant symbolizing nature, a pillow with a golden cover which I made a couple of years ago after a meditation. A few more special memories: a card given to me from a dear friend on my birthday nine days ago, another card with a blessing, an icon, a candle from church, incense, a diploma from the forgiveness school I attended last year, a giant pine cone from a retreat in France, a piece of wood that I found in a forest in Sweden on a retreat with the church, another piece of wood from another place in Sweden, a calendar I got from friends, a piece of cloth with Ganesha from India, and a small book with teachings about walking meditation by a Buddhist teacher.

On the way to the flat, I drove to a flea market looking for a lampshade. There were two perfect ones. I also spotted an orange colored letter L, a perfect symbol for my new flat; L for Lisbeth, L for love and L for Listening, a reminder to keep me front and center in my life, listening with love. Then, I bought some soup to eat as a welcome home dinner.

Welcome home to me.

So here I was in the flat, stepping in for the first time, feeling a bit tense. Walking around with sharp eyes, seeing everything in a new way. Feeling the air slipping in through the window and underneath it. Two bulbs were missing in the kitchen sink lights; the wall in the kitchen wasn't cleaned properly, I see a few spots on the parquette floor, nails still in the wall. Uh! I felt as though I had made a huge mistake buying this flat. I felt a big fear of asking people over, a fear of being questioned on my decision on buying particularly this flat, a decision that I had made all by myself. I felt useless. I heard the voices of children playing soccer outside. It echoed louder and louder. I wasn't able to see or hear the joy in their play. I could only hear my own disturbing thoughts. Was it the crack in the illusion that I could see – again?

Regrets tried to dive into my system but I knocked myself out of the bubble and started to walk around the flat with the incense as a cleaning ceremony; Cleaning out all the old from the place making it all mine and refreshing it. I decorated a shelf with the things I had brought with me, putting the golden pillow on the floor. Eating the soup I brought. Yuk, it was slimy and salty. *Oh no! My perfect welcome dinner was spoiled,* one side of me was thinking. *Never mind,* the other one said. I remembered that I had a plastic bag with some nuts in my rucksack. Perfect. So the meal didn't turn out as I expected. So- I don't have to have opinions of it – a line that I have used a lot during the last year attending a forgiveness school.

Saying Goodbye

Today we signed the selling contract of our old flat. It was sold after two views and being out on the market for only two weeks. We got a great deal. My partner and I met at the real estate agent office. He was standing outside waiting for me, just as he was doing the first time we met 16 years ago. I felt a stab in the heart and a sadness flushing through my system in a millisecond. Discovering our big love fading away over the years, killed slowly by the sweet odor of all the visits of the horrible uncle.

The final decision to end our relationship was made four months ago. It was a mutual decision with both of us knowing that this is what needs to happen; both of us drowning and taking the other part down with us. Not much life left in our systems, neither any love. Just coping in our own special ways– day by day, month after month, year after year. The turning point for me was when I really realized with all my body and mind all the time I had given trying to change – him. Wanting him to be different, thinking that it mattered what I did or didn't do and me trying to control his actions and behavior.. It changed one day when I wrote down all the facts for my eyes to see, for my soul to feel. The numbers and years that appeared in front of me were a wake-up-call. A question arose - *Do I want to spend another year like this?* The answer came straight away – NO.

The new beginning

In the past week, I have had the people I love the most in my life as guests in my new home. I have all through my life been surrounded with mess, both materially and in relationships. I have made nests with lots of things around me, trying to protect myself. My interest in cleaning the house has been non-existent. Maybe I have vacuumed 3-4 times a year. Hardly ever invited people over. The times that happened are easily counted on the fingers of my hand. The last couple of years I have slept mostly alone, crosswise in a big bed with a worn out old mattress.

I'm beginning to land in my new flat. I notice that I like to have it clean and tidy. Putting the crystal vase and bowl on the table and enjoying it. In the past week I have used the vacuum cleaner twice! Yes, I am surprised myself. I have even dusted. My self-value has gone up – a great deal. I like to have empty spaces and not have everything out. In preparation of moving I have cleaned out a lot.

Given things away, thrown things away. It has given me energy and has also been painful with a lot of anxiety. Now I have even had an unplanned visitor in my home. We made lunch together. The same evening I had invited friends over. I made soup and served it in the best china. Tonight some of my spirit sisters are coming over for a blessing party. I've invited the priest from church to come to bless my new home. At my side I want my beloved family. Last week, a total stranger via a Facebook page gave me a bed – the same page where I have given a lot of things away. Now I have a nice thick cozy mattress and I made the bed with fresh linen.

My body is returning to life. My period has been away for over a year. Last week it came by to say hello. The love for life is returning slowly. Fresh air is running in my veins. I recall a sentence I heard a couple of years ago. "Be the change you want to see in the world." It's never too late to let magical things happen in your life. Every trip of ten thousand miles starts with one step. Mine has just begun.

Lisbeth is a certified Qigong teacher and a relaxpedagogue with great knowledge in how to help yourself to inner peace. She likes going on retreats and one of her dreams is running a retreat center of her own. Nature is a deep provider and nurturer for Lisbeth. She is deepening her knowledge in herbs and edible wild plants and sees that as a natural ingredient at the center as well as in her home. Lisbeth has worked as a theatre producer in Malmoe, Sweden for 15 yrs. Lisbeth is also a singer and likes to sing mantras as well as ballads.

Story Twelve

The Curse of Kindness

Charlotte Rudenstam

I kneel in front of him. I literally kiss his feet and I say:

  – *I love you from the depths of my heart, and even if you leave me I will feel gratitude for our love.*

He looks at me from a distance, as if my words don't really concern him.

There is this moment, when I really want him to see me, where I am not kneeling in front of him, where I am not trying to show him the grandeur of my love. There is this moment when I have given up the idea of reaching into him. It's this moment when I am so desperate to be seen that I am prepared to show myself without any disguises, where I am prepared to be seen as a fool or as stupidly weak.

The night before we had had one of our eternal battles, our inner children crying and begging to be seen, and my inner child with a feeling of being beaten to the ground because his inner child demanded all the space. I could see myself trying to console him, leaving my own needs to be left behind because his inner child cried higher than mine. As usual I lost the battle. I ended up surrendering to his inner child; to the stubborn, angry, envious and blaming child in him, surrendering to his needs and in this sequence, abandoning my own inner child. Again.

But in this moment, in the twilight of the morning, my inner child is tapping at my back. She is screaming. She is in rage. She wants me to stand up for me, and she needs me to do that, in some kind of confrontation with him, my husband. The night before, before my surrender, I had really tried to be visible to him. I had tried to get his consolations, his love and his commitment to me and to us. I had failed, as countless occasions before. I had failed. And now I stand there in the twilight. I am desperate. I know that my words don't reach him. I know that me kneeling in front of him doesn't reach him. I know that me massaging his feet with essential oil doesn't reach him. But what would?

My inner child demands action from me. She wants me to show her that she is important. She wants me to prove my love to her. And she yells at me that it's necessary to do that through waking him up.

I am devastated. I am exhausted. I speak to him, and he answers as if not hearing me, not noticing my desperation inside. I stand there in my robe. I walk into the bathroom. I put on the cold-water tap. I shower in ice cold water. Then I go out in to the hallway and stand there. My robe dripping cold water into the carpet. I feel the cold cloth towards my skin. I stand there; eyes closed, in a silent, wet, freezing, meditation.

He doesn't act.

I stand there for five minutes, until my body starts to warm up. Then I go into the shower, cooling myself. Out in the hallway again. Silence. Dripping. No response.

After another five minutes, time for ice cold shower again. Still no movement, no words, nothing from him. I have decided to do this ritual until I get some sort of response. I do this to tell my inner child that I hear her. I am prepared to be this drama queen, to exaggerate this much, to make her understand that I do love her, I am not just there to give him love, to make him feel good. I need to be there for me as well.

It takes more than fifteen minutes for him to react, for him to undress me, for him to give me a warming hug. And it was worth it. It was a way for me to tell my inner child that I am important, that a love relationship is about both people being in a relation, not just one of them.

I have lead groups for ages. Often I start by saying: Be kind to yourself. I've always had a hunch that this "being kind to" is really about me, being kind to myself. The other day I suddenly realized something new. I realized that kindness could be a curse:

Look at this woman kneeling in front of her beloved. Look at her begging him to acknowledge her love for him. Look at her willingness to give him anything to get a response from him.

Look at me, a sucker for love and recognition. Look at me who also want him to show his love for me, in a way body and soul understands.

Look at me who never dared to show my weakness to him nor to anybody else.

It feels like years have passed since that morning. We have decided to divorce. There is a mixture of sorrow, of grief, of gratitude and of love in the air. I am lying on the sofa, beating my head against his body, the man I need to leave and it's like I don't need to be kind anymore. I don't need to pretend I am not weak anymore. I don't need to hide anything from him anymore. In this moment, when I am on the doorstep, it's possible to let him see me in total misery. I am speechless, defenseless, my whole body shaking, and I surrender to my weakness. In this moment I am grief, despair and would rather die, than take another breath.

He holds me. He forces me, with compassion, to look into his eyes. He helps me to stay grounded. He asks me to breathe. He is there in all his mature masculinity. Slowly my body calms down; the panic dissipates. I am lying in his arms, tears rolling down my cheeks. When leaving the house the first time I get panic attacks. He is there. Holding me. When coming back to get my things, we work side by side and when my panic comes, he holds me, steady, and I am safe. He holds me. He is grounded and even he is taken by his sorrow, his pain, and his tears.

It's like it's manageable and safe to show him my uttermost humiliation. Soon I will be living on my own and he cannot question my signs of weakness, nor confront me with it. Maybe this – being caught being weak – is my worse case scenario. I wonder what I can learn from giving into being, for a while, in states of weakness, of hopelessness, of having no control, of not knowing where to put my foot next. I can note a tendency to transform weakness to something else. I prefer to talk about vulnerability, or classify weakness as strength, instead of just owning it.

But still, in this process of separation, we are naked in each other's presence. We admit weakness. We show tears and panic. We comfort each other. Compassion is there. It's like our field of love is stronger than the last couple of years; now when it's time to leave each other. How would my life be, what would I become if I allow weakness to be a part of me? Could that be one crucial missing piece of the persona I call 100% Charlotte? Through my life I have considered myself as being a good girl. I have seen how the good girl in me has served me and made me stumble and trip at times. I have seen how she has tried to do things to deserve love. Now I get in contact with the kind girl in me. A persona who has worked undercover, who has been invisible to me, and who is a much needier kind than my good girl.

Kindness. Sometimes I have loved this quality, and sometimes I have despised it. I once had a very nice and kind boyfriend, and it triggered the bitch in me. I didn't have the capacity to receive his loving kindness. I turned him down. I laughed at him. I was very arrogant. Now I am able to see his love and his willingness and my own incapacity to being loved and how I needed to flee from his love.

His kindness hurt me. And maybe, just maybe, I felt a bit manipulated by his kindness. Maybe I felt that behind this kindness lured a neediness I really didn't like? Or that this reminded me of something I didn't really want to get in touch me? An old wound still sore; I guess I hid my weakness behind a veil of kindness.

Now it's possible for me to see how I have used kindness to get love. It's possible for me to see that it wasn't acceptable for me to be needy – showing weakness – so I chose the kindness strategy. Until now I have been totally unaware of this pattern. How one quality in me can disguise something else, something deeper, something that would hurt more to dig up and scrutinize. I have used kindness to get love. I have hoped that my care and kindness would give me love in return. I have traded kindness for love. To give in to my weakness would be worse than dying. It produced a fear of annihilation.

I have an epiphany around kindness. That kindness has been a curse in my life. That kindness actually has separated me from myself. I realize I have learned that being kind to another is the most important. I have learned that another person's sorrow, shortcomings, grief, and challenges have been more important than mine. That being kind to myself would be to be egoistic. And in consequence with that, self-love is something to be suspicious about.

And now when my husband no longer is my husband, but a very loved man, at a physical distance, I am able to see that it's okay to be weak. It's okay to share responsibilities. It's okay to sometimes lean towards another; and it's okay not to have all the answers. I got the message in the very last months of our marriage. What could have happened if I had included my weakness into our lives together? It doesn't work to get love from being kind, if there is this hidden agenda: "If I am kind to you, you will give me love in return."

I need to start out from myself; giving me love, and then spreading it to others. I need to change perspective. I need to change focus. And I am so surprised. I thought that I already had done the homework.

And I here I stand... knowing what is necessary to do:

> *I need to be kind to me.*
> *I need to surrender to being weak.*
> *I need to listen to my inner voice.*
> *I need to listen to my heart.*
> *I need to say no to what doesn't serve.*
> *I need to say yes to that which serves.*

And it scares the shit out of me.

Charlotte Rudenstam works as a writer and coach focusing on relationships and sexuality." Love is my religion", states Charlotte, and her passion is to spread words of love, sex and freedom to the world. As a coach, Charlotte meets her client in total presence, and has the ability to inspire her clients to live their potential, including their sexual energy. She lives in Sweden.

Be inspired by Charlotte in her blog lustochliv.blogspot.com (some blogposts in English), www.charlotterudenstam.org or www.encourager.se You can reach Charlotte thru social medias like Facebook, Twitter (Lustochliv), Instagram. Email: charlotte@lustochliv.se

Story Thirteen

Codependent to Interdependent

Ingrid Banheden Breisner

For 18 years I stayed in this relationship. We had two lovely children and we created a beautiful home in this marvelous four-winged, half-timbered farmhouse from the 19th century, situated in the countryside. Our living became our lifestyle. We took very good care of this old farm and renovated it the old-fashioned way with materials that suited the style. He was an explorer of life, with lots of energy. Nothing was too hard or too difficult. He could work for hours building our home, and get up very early the next morning, continuing working. Strong and powerful. Life was nice, he loved me and our children but somewhere I felt that we lived on a thin thread. I had unconsciously, or was it deliberately, chosen a home quite far from neighbors, so we wouldn't be disturbed or people wouldn't notice what was going on.

Gradually I realized that we had strict routines and special times for eating and sleeping, of course for the children, but just as much for him; to keep him in balance. I started to stay home in the evenings not daring to leave, because I wasn't sure what would happen to the children when I wasn't there. He was a borderline. From the beginning, I found this all charming the adventures we had! The amazing things we did! His eyes sparkling with joy, life and spirit whatever we did. But these adventures never ended, which became very noticeable when we were a family. We couldn't just explore the world like we did when we were young. We had responsibility to other people, our children, and he felt so too. And yet...

We talked and talked and tried to find a solution, to get out all this energy that was swirling around inside him more and more uncontrollable. Maybe he would try a sport or meditate, qi-gong? My suggestions were boundless and my concern for him preoccupied my mind. He didn't want to take any medication, or get help from specialists. Instead, he self-medicated with alcohol, in the beginning on the sly. These moments of drinking became more and more frequent. He changed. When I told him about his behavior when he was drunk he asked me to videotape him because he could absolutely not believe me. He remembered nothing. I saw another glimpse of him. I couldn't control it anymore. He was beyond and away where I could follow or understand what I was facing. He changed character. From being my lover and best friend he turned to someone I couldn't rely on anymore. The secrets I told him, he misused in a most horrible way when drunk. I became mute, both physically and mentally.

There was a time when every day was decided at 5 pm when he returned from work. Would it be a good or bad evening? When seeing him approach our house I could already determine what the evening would look like, by his looks, so far away. Good or bad. A soft, nice evening or an endless night of talking and accusing from his side and me listening, words with the only purpose to hurt. Those evenings, my only wish was to take all the bad things for myself, and keep him away from the children. If I gave him my time to listen to all this rubbish, he would finally fall asleep all exhausted, and stay away from the children. It could take an hour. It could take four. In my head I told myself that I wouldn't get hurt by his words, that they were mere nonsense, that I was only there but not really listening. I was so wrong. Every single word found its way into my body, into my cells and got planted there. But at that time I didn't understand what impact this had on me. My focus was only on not letting the children be part of this. As time passed, his tongue got more and more harsh, as well as his consumption of alcohol. I told myself that if he ever hit me or my children I would leave instantly. He never did. He hit me with his words instead. He said awful things like I wasn't a good, capable mother as I had had a miscarriage. I was nothing. I was frigid.

I started looking for traces of a mistress. That would be a good excuse for leaving him. I found nothing, only *Miss Alcohol*. Still we had some good moments. I didn't have the strength to leave him, to leave our home, our farm that had become our lifework. I also got used to this thinking that maybe he was right in his accusations and maybe I should be grateful and happy because we had some beautiful moments together. We had lovely children and our home was literally our castle. No one entered it without permission. Our children never brought home friends, except for weekends when life was good. People stopped dropping by without warning. Maybe they knew?

Then, when our son turned fourteen, he started asking questions like, 'when would I tell their father to leave, to leave home and let us live in peace.' "Next week, next week," I repeated. I couldn't imagine myself breaking up from everything. There was still so much attachment. I was also very concerned about what would happen to their father. How would he manage without us? He would be awfully lonely. I was codependent, one hundred percent.

Suddenly I realized and made a decision: what picture would I let my children have of a parent, especially a daughter of her mother? I was always dressed in long trousers and long pullovers. I covered my body with big clothes as a protection. My daughter, who now was seven years old, had heard several times how I was spoken to by my man, her father, the one of only two people in the whole world that she would be able to trust completely. What would she take with her into her relationship if this was the normal one. Finally I decided to leave, to take my children with me with these words ringing in my ears: *it's better to save three persons than letting all four of us perish.* Nothing mattered but my children. The importance of material and beautiful things vanished, and the importance of the farm, which was so much a part of our family history and such a historical monument itself, disappeared. All that mattered was to find a home for my children and me, where we could live safe and calm.

My whole body was blocked for a long time. So many layers of protection surrounded me from getting hurt mentally. My purpose of living the rest of my life was being a good mother, taking care of my children, compensating the bad years they had had and that was that. I felt myself quite old. I was 48 years old at the time and in a way I thought I should be content in life. After all, I had had quite a good life. I had a good job that I liked, two lovely children, some friends. What else could I expect? That was enough for me. I lost ten kilos and I had no idea of what I was going to have my body for: To keep my head on, maybe, nothing more.

One day I got a massage, the sweetest touch I had ever felt for a very long time. My whole body slowly started to melt, to live, to sing, to rejoice and to recognize a feeling deeply buried and protected in me. All the nerves started vibrating, singing, remembering. I cried. Little by little my body woke up after such a long time in lethargy. I reconnected with my body, my temple, my spirit. I became a friend to myself. During my whole life I had travelled a lot, around the world and often off the ordinary touristic tracks. I love exploring new places. Now I started to explore another new place; my inner life and my body and I found a whole universe. I was so grateful. What an amazing world and so close! Suddenly life became an adventure again and age didn't matter anymore. I found THE course; love, lust, life; a four day course where I had time, for the first time in such a long time, to only take care of myself, be with myself, investigate my inner life and feelings, meet my fears, my joys, my sexuality and lust. This course was the absolute step for me to my new life.

I had affirmations all over my new house, met new people with the same idea of living like me. I read books, lots of books, which helped me find the words, the thoughts that were only whirling around in my head. There were other people out there who were thinking like me! I started liking my body, myself and started finding my track. For a while I was quite wild and wanted to test if I could attract men, like a game, flirting around, and yes I could. My life started to speed up. I was in a hurry, wanting to catch up the years I had somehow lost. Everything would happen at the same time. Everything. I turned from inside to outside. I wanted to be everywhere at the same time. Living in a rush. And I wanted to find a new man.

Suddenly I had to stop. An inner voice told me to calm down, that things can't be rushed. Yes, I wanted to meet a new man, for love, but I also knew I could live alone, that my happiness didn't depend on a new man making me happy. I started to believe that I could trust the Universe and if I listened carefully and really wished something, things would come to me. I just needed to have some patience and trust. I got so calm I started listening to my inner voice, doing things I have really loved all my life like yoga, walks in nature, meditation and mindfulness.

And then one day he was there, this handsome and good man, beautiful at heart; A man of my age from the same town as me. We had been in school together but hadn't seen each other for over thirty years. He had divorced recently and we met at a party. In the beginning I couldn't believe him. This was too good. Was it really for me? I had all these strange excuses for not seeing him and was so afraid of trusting him and showing my feelings. He was so determined, patient and calm and seemed to have all the time in the world. I didn't allow myself to just relax and enjoy life. I didn't believe that he could really be nice to my children like that. So I sneaked on him, expecting the worst that he was only nice to the children when I was around. I found no reason at all to be suspicious. I surrendered and let the layers of protection softly disappear, slowly understanding that this was the beginning of a beautiful love story. I could slowly open up my feminine and sensual side again, relax and just bloom. He became my life buoy, steady and reliable, a man that I could count on, no matter what. I brought spirit, creativity, sensuality and a life a bit outside the box into his life.

Last summer we married on the beach, surrounded by our family and closest friends. The sea was singing its soft, sensual song to us and my son was playing wonderful music. There was so much love in the air among all of us. We had good food, lovely speeches and beautiful songs. In the evening, the beach was lit with candles in the sand and the sky was lit with stars. There were no clouds, only the magic full moon of August mirroring on the water, now completely silent.

Our wedding is a symbol of our marriage; natural, sensual, magic and filled with love.

Ingrid Banheden Breisner worked as a teacher for more than 20 years guiding pupils to put words on their thoughts and emotions, in Swedish, English and French. Now it's her turn to introduce her own story. From being a woman concealing her body and voice, her wish now is to help people blooming, reconnecting with their bodies, finding their inner voice, and taking command of their own life, through yoga, writing, sharing and retreats. She believes that everyone has the power within themselves. She lives with her beloved husband in Svedala, Sweden, where they run a health care center, NyttoLiv.

www.nyttoliv.se Ingrid.banheden@nyttoliv.se

Story Fourteen

Witnessing My Self

Renée Jonsson

This is a story about a woman who I know very well that I have not always given the appreciation and love that she deserves in life.

I started to get to know her as a child. She was a lively girl; ready to win every competition she participated in. She loved the spotlight and attention around being the best, both in sports and in school. Early she learned that nothing comes to you easily in life, you have to struggle to deserve either love or happiness. With a mother who was unpredictable and moody, she had to struggle to get attention, but more often disappointment was served.

Her dad was that kind who wasn't around much. When he was, she wanted to steal one of his great hugs that always made her feel safe. When her mom and dad divorced it felt like that security disappeared and she just knew she had to find it again. Not surprisingly she chose to become an actress, her self-confidence was pretty high, but her self-esteem lower.

After a couple of okay relationships, one that gave her a wonderful son, she met a man that really felt like THE ONE. She had always dreamed about HIM, the knight on the shining white horse who was coming to rescue her and sweep her off her feet. She was happy within herself, confident that she was lovable for the first time in her life. He was charismatic, gorgeous, interesting. Everything she had dreamed and hoped for.

They just melted together; their intimate meetings were heavenly. The sensuality their combination awoke in her, made her expand in to her feminine energy, allowing herself to really dive into softness and sexuality. She thanked God every day that he was being so good to her, presenting all this love to give and receive. A love so deep and true it was amazing. The man had two lovely daughters whom she immediately took to her heart as well. Her son got along with the girls right from the start, just like her.

After just a month or two she noticed very strange behaviors with this man, strong reactions she couldn't understand. He showed an odd jealousy about her previous boyfriends and also towards her seven-year-old son. He said everything was about her, that she had done or said something that created all this in him. In the middle of all the love she felt, she started doubting who she was, sensing that there was something wrong with her. Trying to be right, to act right, so that he could feel good about himself and give her love became tiring for her. To show that she was ready to go all in she moved in with him, hoping that would create joy. Behind it all she was lost in the feeling of being with a man she couldn't feel good with. In between the arguments, their love would blossom, for a few hours, maybe days and then her hope grew strong again. Every time the love filled her heart, her doubts disappeared in a flash, and she was convinced they belonged together. But after every one of these moments, her vulnerability expanded, so the next time the reactions took over his being, it hit her to the ground even harder. To protect herself, she was trying to find a pattern in his reactions. But she could see none. It could be anything depending on his daily condition.

After 1.5 years she left him for the first time in total anger; Like a creature reacting when being pushed to the limit. Upset about everything she had put her son through, she moved back to her old apartment. Crying in the disappointment of leaving her "true" love.

The man fell down in a deep hole when she left. He started seeing a therapist to solve the knots inside and reached the point where he could cry for the first time in his life. When she met him, she could feel the transformation. Of course she wanted to give it another try with all the new insights they both had achieved after being apart. The love they felt was clear and her hope was glimmering that they could find new ways to come close.

Soon the destructive energy took up all her time again. Every day was like living in a war zone, fight after fight with no solutions. She started to think she was destined to live in this destructiveness, like it had to be a part of her life. She was blaming herself, both for being there, and for not breaking up. She had started to believe that she was the actual problem that had to be fixed. All the therapy she went through made her even more confused. Feeling there was nowhere to rest. Strangely, the love she felt for him was still there behind the daily struggle.

She left him a second time. A text message was all she could manage to come up with to break up. She was hurt, weak and without energy. It tortured her every minute that she had left like this, that she didn't have the courage to face him. She wrote to him to apologize, to relieve her guilt. This time he was being very friendly with her, telling her he understood she was damaged, that she had traumas from her childhood making her behave like that. She obviously did. It was like she couldn't really think for herself anymore, totally dependent on him. And even if she had felt lost with him, she felt even more lost without him. The natural thing was to go back, trying to make up for all the guilt she felt.

Nothing had changed.

After a vacation with the "whole family" she made up her mind to leave again. She wrote him a short mail to break up, knowing that if she had told him face to face, she was going to let him talk her into staying.
This time she was determined to process it all and stay away. She took good care of herself. She met up with all the friends who she had blocked out. There were several of them who had told her they couldn't stand meeting them together, thinking he was extremely egocentric. She felt ashamed about the fact that she had been with such a man. She had a hard time identifying herself as that woman, always considering herself to be strong and independent. To have witnessed herself in the hands of another person's energy made her feel sorry for herself. She cried and cried to clean it all out. And yet, she thought about the

man behind all the messiness, the man she had seen and still loved... She slowly came back to life where she could laugh from her loving heart again. After six months, he contacted her on a hidden number. Since she was feeling good she made a joke about that, talking to him without any fear of getting drawn back. He felt that joy, got carried away with it and wanted to meet to just talk. She ended up in his arms again, longing for that body she knew so well and with a deep desire to connect. After promising him never to leave him again.

This time it was better than ever; For awhile. But she was also aware of her lowered expectations. The longing for love and to be seen had sort of left her. The darkness she felt at times was very scary to acknowledge. She became a shadow of her own self, acting like she was happy and satisfied. Totally powerless in the situation, she started praying to God. She prayed He would somehow find a way to lift her out of this relationship, this situation, since she didn't have the capability herself. She put it in God's hands, telling Him it was out of her own.

Then one day, he got so mad at her for something – one of those things that she should have known better than to say. He was screaming, yelling in her apartment, she calmly told him to stop but it escalated. It was this one particular thing that upset him more than usual, until he yelled - *It's over between us!* He left and slammed the door, so hard the doorframe fell down in her hallway.

This was one week before Christmas and I was sitting on my bed, a bit shaky from all the anger that had been thrown towards me. After just 30 seconds, I felt this enormous relief running through me. It was over! I was free! God had stepped in, helping me, giving me the greatest Christmas gift ever!

This is my story. I am that woman. I chose to live with a man who wasn't able to let his love shine through. A man I couldn't grow with as a woman. Sometimes it feels like a film I have acted in, yet I can identify myself as that woman now. Embracing her, healing her from within, for all that she put herself through, in the name of love.

I want to believe that this all happened for a reason. For me to see that hurt little girl inside who struggled so much for love and attention, it made her return to a non loving environment in the safety of the attention. Now the struggle is over, and I have made a promise to myself to always take care of my needs. It's going to take time to heal totally and to believe in love again. Sorrow is still overwhelming at times. The sorrow for the fact that I couldn't reach a person I loved and the sadness of the insight that hope can actually be an enemy.

The love I feel for myself right now is tender and soft. It's almost like I'm a newborn. Being on my own helps me awaken the light I have always had inside. My gratitude to God, universe and life itself is larger than I've ever imagined possible. I got help when I really needed it, and so can we all! Leave it in the hands of God!

Renée's gift and devotion in life is to touch people emotionally. As an actress she works with interactive theatre where the audience is participating, to change and affect what happens on stage. Renée and her two colleagues are tools in a creative way to give people aha experiences. She also works as a drama teacher in very diverse groups. She loves to inspire others in every possible way. Awakening people through laughter and recognition, so that they can learn more about themselves and grow; a talent she is constantly developing. www.reneejonsson.se

Part Four

I AM Sensation

"When all is said and done, we exist only in relation to the world, and our senses evolved as scouts who bridge that divide and provide volumes of information, warnings and rewards."

~Diane Ackerman

Story Fifteen

The Legacy of a Lake

Sandy McDougall

Every child is born a naturalist. Her eyes are, by nature, open to the glories of the stars, the beauty of the flowers, and the mystery of life.
~ Ritu Ghatourey

I spent my childhood summers in a small cottage on the edge of a peaceful northern lake. Several other family houses were flung like pearls at intervals along the same shoreline. Many of these were sprawling old country homes built to accommodate ample families of children and grandchildren. My summers revolved around that small clear lake and the north woods surrounding it, and I roamed free in the beautiful surroundings.

The lake was the heart of our life. During the brief and precious weeks of northern summer, my siblings, my cousins, and I spent countless happy hours swimming, playing, jumping, and diving in the water, and around boats, docks, and rafts, every day, rain or shine. Summertime for us was synonymous with communal time in and around the lake.

In the relaxed rhythm of summer, many adults took a little quiet time immediately after lunch. We children were strictly forbidden to swim without adult supervision, so we learned to entertain ourselves during the early afternoons, reading books, and playing cards and board games.

The summer I was nine, an unusually hot and muggy front from the deep south moved far north for a day, pushing away our familiar crisp clear northern air. After lunch that day, even the children joined the adults in quiet time, napping on their beds or daydreaming in their screened porches. It was then that I found myself completely alone, standing outside, barefoot and in my bathing suit.

Mindlessly, I wandered over the empty green lawns to a small, shaded, sandy beach I seldom visited. I was quite aware that I was not allowed to swim, and I had never before broken this taboo. But this was a different kind of day and I felt called to explore new territory. I also yearned for relief from the heat.

Alone on the beach, I gazed out at the water. The lake had transformed under the weight of the southern air. It lay hidden, mysteriously dreamy and deep under the mirrored surface, drawing me in. Slowly and tenderly, I waded into the shallows, which enveloped my legs more like warm cream than water, more smooth than silk. Then, easing gently down on my back at the point where the water was just deep enough to do so, I let my entire body float a few inches above the smooth white sand. And once horizontal, I lay with limbs outstretched, only my eyes, nose, and mouth above the water line. I closed my eyes and relaxed, floating and breathing.

Slowly, the world as I had known it melted away, slipping gently somewhere vast and silent. For a time beyond measure, the edges of my body merged with all else, and I no longer sensed where "I" ended and "all else" began. I was embraced by a sea of warm welcoming peace, aware only of my breath and the exhilarating sense of an astonishingly blissful connection to the lake, to the earth, and even to the universe.

In those delicious moments, I grew wise beyond my nine years. I had become privy to a great secret. There are worlds beyond our immediate knowing to which our body is a gateway. A wise and loving awareness exists both through and beyond our physical being.

The lake had offered me my first conscious sacred experience. All that had previously felt heavy on my shoulders, rough on my soul, dark in my heart, evaporated gently away. Their dissolution created in me a ripple of relief, an exquisite light and lightness, a joy beyond all other joys, and an ecstatic letting go. A bright and luxurious breath of love warmed and enveloped me. Perhaps for the first time since being in utero, I felt infinite peace.

Looking back, I have come to appreciate this and the countless other formative experiences that came to me through my childhood summers by the lake. My lake years are much more than just a lovely memory. I felt grounded and completely at home there. I knew unconditional love and acceptance there. Although I can never go back, the lake is forever a home base for me, a major root in my life, and one of my greatest teachers.

By its shores, I become highly attuned to subtleties in the natural world. Even as a very young child, I observed, with great curiosity, the changeable moods of the water, its ever-shifting temperatures, textures, shades, and sounds. The lake engaged my feelings - wonder, courage, receptivity, sensitivity, eagerness, tenderness, and joy, to name just a few. The lake connected me to life, love, and spiritual depth well before I had language to articulate these things.

Likewise, the lake was my earliest teacher of stillness. Its peaceful spirit called me to daydream, to meditate, and simply to be. The lake was my secret lover. The lake was my secret haven. Many a time, I escaped to the lake for shelter, for safe harbor and source of solace. I reveled in its beauty, purity, peace, and patience. I was enthralled by its many mysteries. Alone by the lake, I could and did look deeply at - and drink fully of - my life and the life around me.

From the lake, I could ask for what I needed and, quietly and over time, I received so very much. The more I paid attention, the more I found. I discovered a world of endless enticing secrets under the water - sunfish basking, minnows playing, snails in their shells, shimmering underwater shadows and golden beams of sunlight through clouds of bubbles. As I uncovered the wealth of life, so near yet hidden away in that fascinating underworld, it first dawned on me that there must be layers of life and beauty hidden around us everywhere.

Summers were my time to explore. I absorbed sensations from sunrise each morning and all the long day until the Milky Way reappeared at night. I can conjure up many wonderful details. And I often do. The thoughts of these things are still so sweet they can bring me to tears.

Life by the lake contained a vast and enticing world, but I myself rarely felt contained. I lived in a strong young body, pulsing with energy. I expressed my physical yearnings in the safe and expansive playground the lake provided me. I could be as active and engaged as I desired and I challenged myself regularly to reach new limits. Could I swim full speed all the way across the lake? Dive from the highest diving board? Canoe against a strong wind? Leap into the water after the first frost in November? I searched for new experiences and new horizons every day.

While my girlhood years comprised a healthy physical contact with nature and the outdoors, few young girls in my day were given permission, encouragement, nor many outlets to live so fully in their bodies. I grew up quite unselfconscious about my physical strivings, knowing neither shame nor judgment about those things. I loved it all wholeheartedly - the surge of sweat, the strain in my muscles, the pounding of my heart.

By contrast, the lake offered me many relaxed and sensual times as well. How often I lay bare skinned in the sun, skinny-dipped under the stars, played naked in the rain, or walked barefoot in the mud. These times nurtured in me a deep and abiding joy and trust in the world. Now when I lose myself in stress, challenge, or busyness, I use the memories of these sensations as a trusted compass to guide me back to myself.

The lake also taught me early on that being alone is not the same as being lonely. I never felt lonely by the lake. As I muse on the lake as my teacher and guide, I also sit in wonder at my possible alternate realities. What might have been my fate had I not had such an expansive and safe arena in which to channel my natural flow of energy, my curiosity and joie de vivre, my dreams and desires.

As comfortable as I was in navigating the natural world, I was a quiet and reclusive child, still somewhat uncomfortable in the social world. I rarely felt playful or open in my personal relationships. When not outdoors, I often turned to books or music. In another world, I might have been the kind of young person who engages in risky or unhealthy physical behavior or who uses excess technology as a kind of escape. Fortunately, my lake environment offered me a home, which was engaging, safe, real, and sometimes, as at the beach that one day, even divine. My life was full. I needed no other diversions.

Ours was a loving, intimate and long-time relationship, my lake and me. Over the years, I became so deeply familiar with the surrounding terrain that I could have walked much of it blindfolded. All these years later, I still carry much of the topography inside me. I can visualize the nooks and crannies of the entire lakeshore, navigate the details of the diverse terrain, re-live the sights and sounds as vividly as if I were still there.

I worry a lot about the future for children in our world. What about inner city children? What about pre-schoolers who spend their playtime on blacktops, or worse, never go outside for recess? What happens if children never know a healthy and natural outer world experience? Does this mean they miss a whole inner imagination and sensual vocabulary within their bodies? What are the implications as they grow up? And what about our collective future?

I have certainly felt great nostalgia for those old times and places. But it has taken me till now to dig a lot deeper. Recently, as I revisit my memories, I have experienced overwhelming floods of gratitude and immense joy. And sometimes, those happy feelings flip over, bringing a rush of intense sadness, a dark loss and deep grief.

In the end, my lake years are a life long touchstone for me. Now I search for a life path that returns me to that place of peace and unconditional love I knew so well. I want that sense of freedom back, and an expansive life full of possibility. I remember the wonder, the gratitude, the dreaming, the striving, the exploring, and how exciting and full my days were. I feel it in my body. No hurry. No worry. Knowing that I was enough. Knowing the world was there for me.

For many years, I thought those feelings would stay with me. Now I know I must be actively and continually cultivating them every day to keep them alive. Over the years, I have unknowingly let them fade. Now it is my intention to wake up every morning and remember the teachings I know, and which root feelings I want to connect to. When I remember, I know exactly where home base is for me. And then I continue on my journey with focused intention, and I choose my way with more clarity, courage, and creativity.

Now, my childhood is long gone. The lake and its surrounding are also gone, forever changed and no longer available to me. But my northern lake taught me very early on that we all have within us and around us miraculous sources of wisdom, bliss, peace, and love. I feel such gratitude to know and trust in this truth. And this knowing has become the foundation of my most intimate, personal, sensual, and sacred experiences.

Sandy McDougall coaches women ready to reclaim their clarity, courage, creativity, vitality, and unique sense of purpose. Sandy believes that nurturing our connection to the natural world helps us remember our loving hearts, our deepest desires, and the highest missions we have on the journey we each call "our life."

Sandy is devoted to family, friends, great food, eclectic books, dancing from the soul, and all things outdoors. She can organize anything and writes about everything. She is always ready to speak to groups. Some of her favorite words are journey, curiosity, full expression, connection, and her current favorite – harmony.

www.themaverickedge.com
https://facebook.com/themaverickedge

Story Sixteen

I Will Survive the Landslide with Chocolat and Ou La La

Alecia Caine

Alchemy

I feel hurt but it's nothing making dark chocolate truffle won't cure.

I follow my passion, the alchemy of working with chocolate. I push aside the betrayal from earlier in the day and turn my attention to the process. I know its healing effects. Part chemistry, part art, infusing my energy into the chocolate and being infused in return. It is like a loveliaison that always satiates and never betrays. Dark, sweet, bitter, luscio

As I practice my new art of making chocolate truffles, my first attempts are clumsy. My energy is sludgy and transfers to the ganache, a mixture of hot, heavy cream, droplets of sweet honey from Southwest France and dark, melted chocolate. The mayonnaise-like consistency breaks. The coverture is too grainy, I must have shed a tear in the liquid sauce that caused it to seize.

I cannot push through this and force it. Mustering up the confidence to begin again, I take the time to create the mood, lighting candles and playing an Erik Satie record. The melancholic, repetitive melody steadies my hand. This time I measure more chocolate and the ganache holds firm. I am steeped with love and passion as I spread the melted chocolate over the uncut layer. The cold ganache stiffens the chocolate cover and now it's ready to slice.

I draw out my long chef's knife and deliberately, yet gently, cut strips horizontally, then diagonally. Each piece is shaped slightly irregular but that's what makes them different. This is not some cookie cutter, industrial mission. Each is unique and special. Authentic. I delicately pick one up with my fingers and dip it in my bowl of melted, tempered, intense chocolate. I allow it to surrender in complete submission into the creamy goodness. Partially submerged, I gently pull it out with my tool and tap it up and down to release the excess sticky goo. I lay the glistening truffle on its rubber sheet and casually sprinkle some magic cocoa powder and salty grains of fleur de sel. It hardens again. I pick one up to taste. Holding it close to my nose, inhaling the exquisite aroma, I lower it to my cheek and guide it to my mouth. Feeling it enter, I let it linger there a bit, immersed in the sensual sensations of taste and smell and texture. The first nibble penetrates the hard exterior and releases its bitter sweet notes, then the creamy center begins to come on my tongue. I take the whole thing in my mouth, close my eyes and enjoy a moment of sweet ecstasy. Nuances of flavor arise and after I swallow, the pleasure lingers into a deep long climax.

Ahhh, chocolate; bite-sized perfection.

Emptiness

As my children have grown into adults and I grow older, I'm confronted with emptiness. Empty Nest. Raw and naked with no excuses to hide behind anymore. The old patterns emerge and converge and in my vulnerability a so called "lover", a tall, sexy man from my past sends me a text. And out of the blue, I also receive a text from a girl friend from my past, the one who once broke a "sister code," the kind of code breaking between women which is rooted in betrayal. How long has it been since I have heard from either of them? Ten, twenty years? Both reemerge, as if on cue, to take up the space that was created in the emptiness. I hesitate to connect. Why is *she* reaching out to me?

I give her the benefit of my doubts and after 3 hours of catching up on the phone about her family and mine, business and life, she shows her true colors. She pries into my love life. "Who are you seeing? Any crushes from your trips to France?" She insists I accept her request to connect on Facebook, immediately. Rifling through my friend list she finds his name. Her own hesitation conveys her true motives as her hidden agenda is accomplished. She continues to probe, and I can feel a stabbing sensation in my heart. She always wants what I have; or what she thinks I have. I see who she really is in this interaction. Jealousy. Competition. Nothing has changed.

I quickly realized my life was better off without these two so I cut them off. I hear Gloria Gaynor singing in my mind: "Walk out that door! Just turn around now you're not welcome anymore…."

Betrayal

Ongoing heart pain that began when I was a young girl from feeling compared and resented by my mother. I remember so vividly, the time my father bought me a beautiful sweater. I cherished it so much and I felt so special, like a princess, until my mother returned it. The pain, the confusion, set up a pattern of feeling unworthy and undeserving and I blamed her. Now, I'm ready to let go of this story and forgive. I realize she wasn't always to blame and I put my father on a pedestal. He and I were so close; in my eyes, he could do no wrong. But I see that story is incorrect, too. As I developed into my own person, I discovered that he wasn't completely innocent but could be controlling and manipulative as he conspired against my mother, my sister, and even tried to manipulate my owns sons against me if he saw me living my own life and not the life he wanted for me. I can still love them both knowing that they are not perfect and I stand in my own truth that my desires and my dreams and my hopes are mine and no one has the right to take them from me.

Compassion

I now understand, my parents' unexamined pain of abandonment caused them to lash out unconsciously, continuing the abusive patterns that began way before they were even born. The pain their parents' parents must have endured is anyone's guess but surely their inherited grief played out generation after generation causing a legacy of psychological wounds that I am determined to shift. I bring light and forgiveness to our history and the hope to unravel, arrest, and refocus this legacy, undoing and hopefully preventing future scars and begin new patterns of love, compassion and healing.

Shame

At the tender age of 21 and still unaware of these destructive patterns, the theme of betrayal continued in my marriage to a narcissistic, angry, young man who would stomp out the beauty in my young heart. A man who was so badly abused as a boy that all he could feel was his own pain as he emotionally abused those who loved him most, belittling and putting down his family. When we were newly married, I was still in school and he was shipped off to Europe to serve in the military. Later when I joined him, he unloaded his conscience and told me about all the women he had slept with. Knowing he contracted the herpes virus, he didn't even bother to keep me safe and he transmitted it to me. The physical pain never compared to the years of shame I have endured, the fear of rejection, the settling for whoever will have me since I was tainted. But the turning point was the physical abuse he inflicted on our son that woke the sleeping fierce lioness within me as I rose up to protect my children and myself.

Uncovering Me

In present time, I see my sons grown into happy loving young men, flourishing in their chosen life paths and in healthy relationships and I know, with all my heart, that I have shifted the negative tides. But my work isn't over. It is time to shift this back to me. I see the patterns I have broken for my sons. What else can I uncover for me? Where have I been hiding and putting up with the agenda of other people. The patterns of betrayal persist in less obvious but nonetheless insidious ways in waves of so-called friends and lovers who have drifted in and out of my life leaving a path of pain in its wake.

But the worst kind of betrayal and the one I am looking at head on now is self-inflicted. The way that I betrayed and continued to abandon my own dreams and desires; always putting others needs ahead of my own. I don't mean raising children, that's a noble cause for putting personal aspirations on hold while focusing on what's important, but I was good at hiding behind my role as mother as an excuse to put my desires on the back burner.

In my "emptiness" the dreams and desires are awakening in waves.

Passion

Visions of Eiffel towers flood my memory, I look around and I see that powerful symbol everywhere. It's on the quilt I chose as a bedspread, in pictures of Paris that adorn my walls from Picasso to Chagall. Books and paperweights, even potato chip bag clips are all Eiffel towers. Ah, there must be a clue here, ya think? Following my desires, scary at first, I booked my first trip to France in many years. A trip for myself to explore my senses, my long lost dreams, my long lost self. Finding myself there as I walked the quaint cobblestone streets, tasting wine, sipping champagne, tasting morsels of cheese, fresh baked breads and pastries and yes, loads of luscious chocolate. A passion. I followed this passion. It held me, conjured my dreams of being a princess in a chateau, my gallant knight taking me by night... I began to find myself. I found love for me and all things I love.

And then I returned to California. Not sure of what was next. People from my past returning to tempt and tease me. In the emptiness, I begin to stay with these questions. What's next? What did I once long for? And how do I long to be touched, loved, made love to now?

Being drawn in for only a moment, I say no to the old temptation. My vibration is higher and I've learned my lesson. I only want authentic true love and friendship. Life is too short for anything else.

I return to the chocolate truffle, a luxurious pleasure filled with my passion. A metaphor for making love. The alchemy of the chocolate is awakening my desire. And this time, I am molding and shaping the chocolate into my dreams and desires.

The pleasure. The ecstasy. The desire is all mine.

Alecia Caine is a modern day renaissance women. As a CPA and single mom, striving for work life balance in a male dominated profession, Alecia discovered her own path for success and created Moulala to empower and inspire women to live life to the fullest with joie de vivre while achieving financial success. A lover of travel, Alecia founded Find Your Self in France, designer of bespoke itineraries to France. After raising her 2 sons, she is following her passions from France to chocolate making, travel writing and more recently to Italy where she will live part time. www.moulala.com
www.FindYourSelfinFrance.com

Story Seventeen

Follow Your Bliss

Louise Weibull

My partner and I start the New Year by making love.

Last time we became one with our bodies intertwined was so long ago. I can`t even remember. After years with almost no intimacy I have slowly grown to long for making love again; longing for the masculine and for the feminine. I`m longing to feel my body, longing to feel warm, juicy, wet, tingly, awake and alive.

I am opening myself up to him. I am showing him that I want him, that I am willing, that I am not keeping him outside in the cold. I can see the love in his eyes. I can see his desire, his longing for being allowed to love me, to get close to me and love me from his lust as a man. He loves when I embrace the woman in me. It turns him on; my body, my eyes, my sparkle, my curves. I know he takes in every moment, every touch. I know because I haven't let him near me for years.

I am changing. I have changed. I have chosen to embrace my femininity and body once and for all. For a very long time, my reaction to sexual invitations was anger mixed with shame and guilt. I had closed down my whole system. Men were predators that I had to protect myself from. But maybe the truth was that I was my own predator. Inside me lived a woman with desires. There lived a whore, a Madonna, a girl and a wise woman; All of whom suffered deeply when I closed myself off from sex and intimacy.

And here we are, New Year's night. I let myself indulge in whatever feeling my body is having. When his lips are all over my breasts, my body gets pulsating and hotter and I feel my yoni coming alive. I am free falling.

I love his attention. I love his careful and sensitive ways with me, his soft hands touching. He knows too well how easy my system closes down. I know how quickly I can shut myself down, if I push myself too fast, if I don't listen to my body and subtle signals. I close down in an instant, being back as a victim that needed protection from the predator.

This evening is different. We have been on a long and challenging journey together in the past and tonight we are so much more conscious. I trust him and myself like never before. And I talk, I whisper. I tell him my fears. I tell him what I like. I gently take his hand and show him what my body yearns for... from him. He is very present. He listens and follows my moves like waves on the water.

Instead of keeping me all in, feeling ashamed, I invite him to my world. Little by little.

I am free falling.

I'm free to be whomever and whatever I want to be. I am free when I feel serious, when I listen within, when I withdraw inwards. I am free to judge myself or not judge. I am free towards whatever inner voice I listen to. I am free when I allow myself and others to feel and be whatever they choose to be.

What happens when I am entering my heart space? What does being free feel like then? When did I last feel free? How did that happen and what happened? How am I free when I express my sensual voice and do I feel free when I feel sensual?

I entered my relationship with silent and unconscious expectations of him. Of course I could not see them at first, but as the years passed they turned into projections of my unhappiness caused by him, I thought. He didn't heal my wounds. He didn't give me back my own feeling of worthiness that I lost sometime in my childhood. And of course I didn't meet his unconscious demands on me either. We lost our love among our wounds we carried with us from the past. We argued, blamed, felt misunderstood and victimized each other in our so-called union.

To love from my heart is totally different than to love from my ego. When I later chose to lick my wounds instead of telling him how wrong he was, then he had the courage to relax and examine his own. One lesson learned is that we cannot fix each other but give space and witness each other's willingness and growth. My little daughter's six-year-old friend once told her mother, "a heart that is soft cannot be broken." How wise our children are.

I understand that if I want to be sensual, be happy, be that creative soul I am born to be, I need to connect. Connect with life, with my partner, with my creativity and the most important to connect with myself. It does not need to be expensive or complicated. It can be a walk in nature, cooking a nice meal, feeling creative, going swimming, visiting the local art center.

I am my tool in this life. No one or nothing else. Simple as that.

Two months later on a Friday morning; Spring is in the air, the ground is covered with snowdrops and winter aconites. The branches are filled with little buds that in a few weeks time will explode and welcome the sought after spring. I am listening to the spring birds through the window as I make myself a cup of tea. The tea bag has a little tag on it with a message. I read "Love is always fresh," and I remember the last walk we took together, he and I, when the ground still was covered with frost.

A blissful moment
amongst the trees.
The ground
a carpet of moss
so soft, so tender

We, me, I and you

together with the woodpecker
the squirrel and our dog

You made me coffee that day
Enjoying your hobo-kitchen
I watched you and my heart was singing
You are wearing that smile of peace.

It started to drizzle
Little tiny, fine raindrops
The dogs' paws raw, red
Soon the cups were empty
Time to go
Your hand in my hand
The winter cold creeping in under the jacket
Walking in silence
Our minds in two different worlds
Re-union in a third.
This.

It is there in the silence
amongst bare trees and a carpet of moss
that I start to see clearly
what it is behind and beyond life,
It is there I hear my heart's voice.

The month of March arrives. It is a full moon
and eleven o'clock at night. I lay down on the
floor in my new refurbished room. I can feel
my body on the wool rug and the moonlight
softly embraces my body through the window.

All lamps are turned off; Only this ancient light around me. He comes and lies down next to me.

I think the love and attraction between us is like a living organism. It needs constant flow otherwise it stagnates or even worse dies.

I have had two stagnated areas in my life: creativity and sexuality. I thought healing my sexuality would heal my creativity. Now I start to believe it might be the opposite (even tougher they go hand in hand). I feel creativity is the foundation that life exists at all. Therefore, I think being connected to my inner creativity is a main power tool of how I respond to living my life. Since I started to nurse my creativity I can feel the flow and the connection to life coming back to me again. This is healing in itself and gives me a lot of confidence and self worth. To look after my creativity gives me lust and more lust to rediscover my sexuality for myself, for my man and for us.

It was through nursing my creativity that I learned love is always fresh because so is creativity. It is just an amazing journey of discovery and it taught me that when I deprive myself from sensuality, from sex or from making love because I feel fear or shame, I deprive myself from living a healthy, fun and joyous life. It is the same when I deprive that creative inner call like writing this text because

I need to cook dinner, or do the wash. I came to a point when I had to raise my own consciousness by looking at myself in that famous mirror. One of the best things I ever did. Painful at times, but the rewards are bigger then I could ever imagine.

The loved ones need light to shine back at their hearts.
To remember what brought them together and not apart.

The trees are standing, the sun is shining
the flowers cover the ground
Embrace the healing that comes from around
It is stronger
than the darkest cloud

Your conscious power
You can never beat
Water it
And clear its wreath.

Blow your mind
Set it free
Open up
Fly to that orbit
you just dismissed
Fly and be free
so you know you exist

Fly and
Be free
so
you
know
you exist.

Follow your Bliss.

Louise Weibull is currently living in Sweden, accomplishing the awakening of her soul mission. For her, photography is a sacred tool of creation and healing. She is an artistic soul always trying to capture the essence and pure beauty in what ever she depicts. After a session with Louise you will walk away with not only professional photographs, you will also have had a moment of healing and connection with self-love. Louise photographs Portraits, business, commercial and Interior design. She is currently working on her own photography book exploring the wisdom of feminine.

Connect with Louise at: *www.louiseweibull.com*

Story Eighteen

Surrender

Sofia Sjöblom

Letting go of control.

Leave yourself in the hands of another person.
Feel the trust.
Feel the presence.
Feel the love.

Feel the ropes that tie you up,
More and more.

Distinctive. Hard. Soft.

A pause
A warm, soft hand touching your chin.
Eyes looking deep into your eyes,
filled with love, care and presence.
The energy that flows in the body,

Surrender to it

Let
it
be
there

And let it be expressed.

The body knows how to express it. There is
laughter. There is shivering. There are tears.
There is total trust and faith. Total surrender.

And what's left is pure love.

*****

At first I didn't know what to expect. There
were two other women who were tied up

before me and when he started with the first one I felt like a six-year-old little child,

"Me too!
I want it too!
Yahoo"

And then I realized that it was quite tough, not only an ordinary play and I was so fascinated. I sat with my eyes wide open, just absorbed with what was going on in front of my eyes. I could hardly breathe. I was totally caught up with what I saw and felt in the room.

There were 20 people in the room. It was totally silent. The only sounds were a swoosh from the ropes when he made a knot and dragged it through the loop and the thud when the end of the rope landed on the floor. And a sigh or a sound of surprise, a gasp from her when he tied the rope quite hard. More and more ropes in a beautiful design as he suspended her so she floated in the air. The atmosphere in the room was so intense, everyone so focused, concentrated and immersed in the artwork that emerged in front of us.

When it was my turn, he connected to me and said it would be a bit different from the others. I was nervous and excited. I longed for the experience and it felt really good just to step right in to it. He helped me let go of everything and to surrender to the present moment. His movements and the feeling of the ropes, sometimes a quick move and the rope was around my body. Sometimes slowly, the rope gently dragging over the skin and all the time, distinctive and firm movements. I could trust him. I could feel he really knew what he was doing.

My whole body shivered. I cried and I laughed. I did not try to keep any feelings inside. I let them flow fully. When he finally untied me, there was a sensation of aliveness in my whole body. It was so sensual. I felt that I showed myself from my deepest being, and I knew that I had been longing to do so for a very long time.

Something changed in me from that experience. I felt like I landed down to earth and deep down inside of me. I was more aware in daily life, more aware of myself, of the energy in my body, more aware of what's happening inside. It opened me up to new rooms inside and I saw myself with new perspectives when old feelings came up in different situations.

I felt that I was finally seen. All of me.

Surrendered.

When I was 14 years old I went to a party that my classmate arranged. We were three girls and three boys. The boys were a little older than the girls and it was so thrilling. It was kind of decided beforehand who should be with whom. We drank something, we danced and had fun and we cuddled and kissed each other. Of course I fell in love with "my" guy. We went on an excursion some days later and it all was so nice. After a while my classmate arranged a new party with the same people invited. I was so happy and joyful to meet him again. But when I got there, I felt that something was wrong. There was another girl, some years older than us, and a guy that was not so popular. It became obvious to me that I was replaced. The new girl would be with "my" guy and I was supposed to be with the less popular one. I was so shocked. I had no idea what was going on. No one had said anything to me. I was totally heartbroken and I didn't understand anything. I didn't want to stay, but I didn't want to go home either. It felt like a big failure to go home early and be so sad. So I stayed in a corner and felt miserable. When I finally went home I felt so ashamed and I had no one to talk to about it.

This situation had a very deep impact on me. I learned that I was not good enough, that no one wants to be with me, that everyone is better than me. Love is not for me. I cannot trust men. I was so ashamed and I learned to hide my feelings deep inside in silence.

And when I wrote about it recently another picture came to me. I have always thought that it was the guy who found me too boring and asked to have another girl. But I realize that it could as well have been the girl's initiative. And I felt a great relief, if it wasn't his wish, maybe I can trust men. And the day I realized that I started to dance with my 14-year old Sofia. So happy, relieved and free.

Surrendered.

Through life I have brought with me two strategies for hiding my inner feelings. One strategy is the impatient one that makes me do a lot of things in a rush. It makes me run through life a bit too fast. I drive myself too hard in a high gear that is not good for me. Doing too many things too quickly and without any pause or relaxing in between. I use too much energy and I get exhausted. This is an efficient way to escape from myself, from avoiding being in the present and from feeling my body and heart. It's difficult to notice when that strategy comes. It arrives so quickly and automatically and in seconds I am there doing things in a great rush. When I do notice it, I can stop and slow down, notice what I feel and then make a decision what to do next. That is a relief.

This year, I decided to cleanse a lot before New Year, emotionally and physically. I went deep down into the center of myself, seeing and experiencing many old patterns and really ugly things. I have never gone so deep before. Some days there was a real turbo going on. I did what I could to just notice, letting it be there, letting the waves of feelings come and go. Different situations occurred in real life to help me stay connected to the old patterns. People I have had no contact with for a long time for different reasons were contacting me and giving me a chance to release stuff. I set my boundaries in some cases, came to a completion in another and became more aware of my needs and what I really am longing for.

When I heard that a man I dated for a short time had met another woman, I was surprised by my feelings of jealousy. I had chosen to stop seeing him but I felt a strong sadness and despair and a jealousy towards the woman who had received what I didn't want.

The other strategy for hiding my feelings is to stand in a corner and watch and listen. Not talking or showing myself, I can feel unsure, don't know what to say or how to start a conversation. Unsure how I will be received, what others will think. Wondering if I am interesting enough. Afraid of not being good enough, not smart enough and that people shall turn their back to me or laugh at me. I can easily get the feeling that I have said something stupid or ridiculous and I'm afraid of the reaction from others.

I recognized that feeling from my childhood. When we talked and discussed things in the family, my parents and my sisters, I wanted to be in the circle and say what I had in mind in the discussion. As the youngest one, they thought it was so "cute" what I said, maybe not so accurate. But it was my thoughts and they laughed at me. I felt so violated. I felt that I had no value and I was nothing. I went from the table and cried and did not want to come back. I know they didn't want to hurt me, but I learned that I had to be very clear and smart in the way I wanted to express myself. I had to think it through very precisely before I said something.

For fear of being abandoned and left behind, I have put myself aside, abandoned myself and just standing there, hoping for someone to see me.

Surrendered

In my new state of surrender I am fearless. Another way of saying it is that there is nothing wrong in feeling scared, just don't let it stop you from doing what you want.

When I have met men in the past, I have been afraid of not being good enough. It made me critical and I saw all things that were wrong with them and made it impossible for us to have a relationship. Now I meet men with a curiosity instead, seeing and feeling him as he is. Without all images of how he should be, I feel free to receive what's coming up.

And I realize it has nothing to do with the men, it's all about me. I was very harsh to myself on the inside. I was never good enough in my own eyes. I was very critical and could not accept all parts of me. Now I know I'm doing my best and that is good enough. I see and feel new aspects of me with curiosity and without the images of how I should be. I feel free, free to be me.

It's like a dance; life itself has invited me to this dance and I like it. Surrendering in the ropes helped me to be courageous enough to surrender to life itself, to just let it be, just let it happen. Surrender and let someone or something or nothing take the lead, without knowing what will come. Surrender to myself. Inside new worlds have opened. Old feelings and blockages have been released. A lot of fears have been welling up. I just stay present and let them be there. It was ok, not too bad. They have ceased and become less intense.

Something has changed in me.
A new kind of presence
My body is swaying when I walk.
A stillness that is open and curious.
A belief there is good in everything.
Life is good to me.
I feel cherished and taken care of.
Grounded and inside myself.
Just as I am,
I just AM.

Humble.

I bow before all possibilities that open up.
With possibilities I say yes to life.
I can be clear with what I want.
It's safe.
I can say yes and no.

Welcome to everything that is.
Feeling happy, calm and grateful for life.
Joy and love that's flowing through me.
From me and to me.
All the time.
Love. Is.
I love.
I am loved.
I surrender to love.
Surrender.
Sweet Surrender

Sofia Sjöblom is a life traveler and explorer who follows the whirls of life with an open mind. Her coaching speciality is helping people to surrender and let go of ideas, structures and struggles, to be free to follow the flow of life here and now. Sofia is also a Breathworker, Teacher at the Breathwork training, A Goodheart Laughter coach, Sensibility coach, Doula, and a Socialpedagog.
www.aifos.se

Story Nineteen

Slut:
A woman with the morals of a man

Andrea Hylen

After my husband died, I didn't have sex for eight years.

I was 48 years old when he died. And if I were to believe what a relative told me when I was 25 years old, my days for sex were almost over anyway. (She told me no woman wants to have sex after she turns 50.) As a grieving widow, sex was the last thing on my mind. My immediate focus and priorities were homeschooling our 12 year old daughter. Selling my husband's business. Taking care of our house on 3 acres with a pool, wood stove heater and gardens. Everything was in upheaval and transition. The details kept me busy and exhausted. And underneath it all I was numb and grieving. Then something changed.

It began when my body started waking up like crazy about 6 years after my husband died. Turned on; Heart racing like a schoolgirl with a crush. Genitals buzzing. There was so much heightened, sexual sensation in my body I wanted to scream. It came in waves and I didn't know what to do with it. I felt like a cat in a bed of catnip so I tried to get rid of the sensation. Masturbating. Dancing. Running. Cold shower. Hot bath. I couldn't control it or stop it.

I knew these were not hot flashes. I entered perimenopause at the age of 45, ten years earlier. I was one of the lucky women to transition easily with the support of B-complex and extra rest. No, this was more like what I had heard was a kundalini rising experience, a primal physical jolt of sexual energy. It can happen when you are in a period of deep spiritual practice and growth. The description fit my daily meditation silent walks in nature and mindfulness practices of deeper listening to my inner voice.

This "awakening" continued on and off for two years until I ran into a friend at the Agape Spiritual Center in Los Angeles one night. After a hug and some basic "how are you," small talk, he asked me to give him a summary of what was happening in my life right now. The words poured out of my mouth. Sexuality. I told him I wanted to talk about it on the radio, write about it and figure out what a "respectable" woman in her 50's was supposed to do with all of this body sensation. I told him I wanted deep physical connection with the lights on. Exploring the desire in my body and I wanted slow, full, rich connection. It felt so good to say it out loud and to admit my desire to a man.

He told me it felt like a powerful conversation to explore and he invited me to dinner with a group of friends. After dinner, we lingered over tea while he told me about a 15 minute partnered practice called Orgasmic Meditation. He shared information about how it was a practice of connection, sensation and attention between a man and a woman. Later that night, I reviewed a video on the OneTaste website, attended a lecture by Nicole Daedone a week later, and signed up for an Introductory How to OM workshop.

Entering into the world of Orgasmic Meditation seemed really natural and it also brought up feelings about wanting to hide this desire; hiding was in direct contrast to the way I have lived my life as an adult, authentic and transparent.

*****

When I was 11 years old, I used to sneak my Dad's Playboy magazines out of the house. Hiding them under my shirt, I would ride my bike to meet my "boyfriend." Our meeting place was outside, on the back steps of an abandoned house. We would look at the magazines in silence; never touching, or talking or kissing. We were curious and there was a desire building in our bodies that neither of us had a clue as to how to express, explore or take action. I knew I wanted his attention and the sensations in my body felt amazing.

When I was 13, my friend Roxane and I climbed under a bridge to meet with some boys she knew. Roxane was always so daring. I have no idea where she met these boys, only that we were there for breast fondling and nothing else. We let them squeeze our breasts over our clothes. It felt good to be touched and at the same time I felt shame around the feelings of wanting to be touched and what a "good girl" was allowed to do. So much confusion around desire, curiosity and what I "should or shouldn't" be doing.

In high school, I used to meet my boyfriend after evening school activities to explore our bodies and have sex in the back of my family station wagon. The electricity we generated and the taste of his lips and sweat felt so natural and real. I longed for his touch and it awakened my desire and connection to everything. The deep touching of my body carried over into every area of my life. It cracked me open to a connection with my voice, leadership, and confidence.

Throughout my adult life, the idea of sexual exploration meant trying different positions for intercourse. There was nothing about looking for deeper connection. Sex was cock sucking; Penis into vagina. Sex always came with a goal to reach climax. Kissing and foreplay decreased in my long-term relationships. It was too vulnerable to talk about desire. In conversations with girlfriends there was more talk about NOT having sex because of the demands of parenting, stress of jobs and earning money, duties in maintaining a home, frustrations with the "men" in our lives. There was an unspoken agreement not to talk about the ecstatic, spontaneous in the middle of the night sex with reverberating climax when it happened. If sex entered any conversation, it was laced with the tokens of romance and flowers and I could feel the women longing to be seen and held.

Inside of me were these different parts that seemed incongruent, the mother, the slut, the nice girl, the bitch, the soft feminine, the determined warrior. Most of the time, I felt like I had to shut down the desires of the slut. I rarely let her take charge and claim her lusty, natural desires.

At the age of 56, I entered a world of sexual exploration consciously and took one step at a time; pausing, trying something new, reflecting, checking in to see how it felt in my body and willing to experience everything. I decided to become a living research project. Over a two-year period, I practiced Orgasmic Meditation (OM) with multiple partners, had an intimacy research partner to explore sex and vulnerable conversation, lived in a conscious community with a morning OM practice, and took a year of coursework in a Desire-based Leadership Program and Orgasm Mastery. I kept a journal to record my experiences and feelings.

*****

OM #28: A moment in an OM

Have you ever had a man place his full attention on your body?

Me, quietly: "I feel sad,"
Him calmly: "I've got you. Let it out."

Laying on my back, legs spread in a butterfly position, his finger lightly stroked my clitoris in this 15 minute partnered practice. This time I released sadness. His attention and my surrender allowed wave after wave of sobbing outbursts to erupt from the cells of my body and through my voice. After the first five minutes, I could feel the sobs welling up again like a wave in the ocean building to a crescendo. I shout out to him:

"DON'T LEAVE ME""

Him, "I'm right here. I won't leave."

In this, my 28ᵗʰ OM (Orgasmic Meditation), I am releasing so much emotion, I cannot believe a man will stay connected, will keep lightly stroking, will hold a space calmly while I get to feel and release everything!

I was raised with the idea that men were incapable of holding my emotion. I had to tone it down. Be a nice girl. Cry silently. Alone. The idea that a man could place all of his attention on me without asking me to immediately turn and place my attention on him is amazing.

After the OM, he asked if I was okay. Did I need anything? Water? Food? Bathroom? Another

OM? Yes to water and bathroom and OM. Get back into the OM nest of blankets and pillows and integrate what just happened.

I lay down in the nest again; legs butterflied open. Trusting him even more. Going into deeper surrender. Throughout the OM, the only thing that emerges is connection, heightened sensation and more pleasure than I have ever felt in my life. I am cracked open.

The experience changed us both. I felt a man place his full attention on me. Holding all of me. And going into the deepest surrender I have ever felt. He experienced a woman trusting him enough to let him hold her, all of her. Maybe the things we were taught about women and men while growing up are not true. We both saw a glimpse of what is possible with greater connection, trust, surrender and support.

He later described me as one of the chambers of his heart. For breaking his heart out of his prison and putting it back together. This was a moment in time that cracked both of us open to be more of who we are in our separate lives. I am grateful that our paths crossed with so much intimacy and healing.

*****

It was so incredibly liberating to live in an environment where I could connect with my body, run my business, live my life fully. I experienced what was possible. I learned to receive more in every area of my life. I kicked my people-pleasing ass to the curb and I felt more like myself than ever before.

After two years of immersion in intimacy and sex research, I packed my suitcase, left the community house and stepped back into my old life. I began to ask myself what's next? Do I want a life partner? Do I want to live in another house with a daily OM practice? During my research I gave the "slut" a voice and experience. I like her. She is amazing and powerful. I want to give her a voice and expression along with all of the parts of me. (The Urban Dictionary describes slut as a woman with the morals of a man. To me that means in our society, men can express natural sexual desire but women receive demeaning, shameful labels that shut down our sexual desires and expression.)

During my exploration, I had written blogs and talked on the radio. I launched the Heal My Voice Sensual Voices writing program and created a 12-week audio course on Sexuality, Power and Money. All of this "sex" talk was upsetting to people I care about. My outspoken candor with sexual exploration was reflected back with anger, shock and disapproval. I could feel the sensual woman confused and shutting down. I noticed the shame I began to feel about telling anyone when I was going to go meet someone for my orgasmic meditation practice or about admitting that having my body touched regularly was important. The reactions were met with winks and sensational comments or judgmental looks. Writing this story helped me process my underlying desire now.

I want to be in a primary relationship with a man who is emotionally mature and has been working on his own personal growth. He has the desire to explore intimacy and connection in a relationship. He is willing to stay connected in the peaks and valleys. We have a daily orgasmic meditation practice with each other. Our sex is dynamic.

Is there a man in the world who is a match to my energy? Someone who is passionate about life, and who desires connection, independence and interdependence? Someone who can hold me exquisitely so I can go into my involuntary and who is also going to play in a new way of living in relationship? Someone who is willing to be vulnerable, expose himself in softness and in strength? I want to be in a relationship with a man who finds me fascinating and knows how to stroke out all of me, my power and brilliance, free-spirited, open heart, playful, and hold me when I am unsure, scared, fearful and doubting.

I know I am ready to give a man the same thing I am asking for: A giving and receiving experience in a dance of infinite flow.

I am ready.

Andrea Hylen believes in the power of a woman's voice to usher in a new world. She is the founder of Heal My Voice, a Writing and Transition Coach and Orgasmic Meditation teacher. Andrea has discovered her unique gifts while parenting three daughters and learning to live life fully after the deaths of her brother, son and husband. She is currently living out of a suitcase following her intuition as she travels around the world speaking, teaching, collaborating and leading workshops. Her passion is authentically living life and supporting others in doing the same. *www.andreahylen.com* and *www.healmyvoice.org*.

Photo Credit: Wendy Mata

Part Five

I AM Loved

"When a woman becomes her own best friend life is easier."

~Diane Von Furstenberg

Story Twenty
(A story in Swedish)

Att älska mig i nöd och lust

Rinella Grahn

Det var en av de hetaste somrarna vi hade haft. Jag låg raklång på bryggan. Den varma kvällssolen värmde min kropp. Framför mig öppnade sig ett vidunderligt landskap som bjöd in till en vigsel mellan mitt hjärta och naturen. Havet var stilla och lät sig vara en spegel för himlavalvets skådespel. Solen höll på att ta avsked av ännu en dag. Här låg jag och upplevde solnedgången som om det var första gången jag hade varit med om den. Plötsligt insåg jag att jag låg på en smutsig båtbrygga i en ren vit klänning. "Så får man inte göra" sa en sträng röst inom mig. En annan röst sa "njut älskade flicka, det gör ingenting om klänningen blir smutsig, det finns tvättmaskin". Flickan i mig slappnade av och tillät sig att njuta ännu mer.

Som barn var jag som en söt docka samtidigt som det fanns en vildunge inom mig. Mamma var från modestaden Milano och klädde upp mig i rosa och vita sidenklänningarna med matchande diadem. Jag lärde mig tidigt att vara till behag för min omgivning. Det var lugnast så. Inom mig fanns en stark längtan efter att vara fri och fånga ögonblicken såsom de var. Att få bejaka kroppens alla sinnen och utforska världen. Att vara nyfiken och gå på upptäcktsfärd. En röst inom mig talade om för mig att det var mitt rätta väsen även om omgivningen begärde något annat av mig. Den starkt livsbejakande vildflickas röst vägrade att låta sig tystas. Istället började hon sakta kapslas in i ett tryggt förvar långt inom mig. En dag när tiden var inne skulle hon åter ge sig till känna.

Då och då fanns det stunder som vildflickan klev fram och blev synlig. Som den dagen då den stöddigaste grabben i femte klass försökte sätta mig på plats för att jag var tjej. Enligt honom skulle tjejer inte ifrågasätta grabbar. När jag ändå gjorde det och inte lät mig tystas på hans kommando, då frågade han mig om jag tiggde stryk. Inom mig vaknade vildflickan till liv och jag svarade att jag var beredd att brottas med honom. Slagsmålet var i full gång när vår lärarinna kom ut på skolgården och särade på oss. Från den dagen hade jag vunnit full respekt hos de övriga grabbarna i klassen.

Vid ett annat tillfälle i övre tonåren blixtrade åter vildflickan till liv. Min vilda längtan efter frihet vann över mitt sunda förnuft då jag en sommardag satte mig på en motorcykel och åkte sträckan Kristianstad - Danmark i bara bikini. Varför skulle jag ha något annat på mig denna varma sommardag undrade jag och hoppade längtansfullt upp på motorcykeln mot en hisnande färd i totalt frihet.

Samma vilda känsla av frihet pulserade inom mig när jag för ett år sedan vandrade upp för ett berg i Italien helt ensam. Då kände jag hur hjärtat dunkade och jag trodde att jag skulle dö. I samma ögonblick som jag kände att mitt hjärta kanske skulle kollapsa, upplevde jag också ett lyckorus. Om jag skulle dö så var det här i detta ögonblick av vildhet och frihet. Det skulle vara ett lyckligt dödsögonblick.

Tidigt ställdes jag inför livets prövningar och utmaningar. Jag blev en expert på att bita ihop och kämpa. Jag lärde mig att göra allting efter givna mallar och utan klagan. Med tiden blev jag mer alltmer allvarlig. Inom mig bodde en barnslig hoppfullhet som önskade att varje utmaning skulle vara den sista. Efter varje sådan skulle livet ge mig utrymme för den lek och lust som jag så innerligt längtade efter. Min följsamhet gjorde att omgivningen förväntade sig att jag fanns där för alla. Och jag lät mig finnas till för alla. Den enda jag inte räckte till för det var mig själv. Jag längtade efter att följa livets flöde men följde istället normerna.

Jag, min bror och mina föräldrar hade efter flera års utlandsvistelse återvänt till Sverige och mina föräldrar försökte ge familjen en nystart. Det krävde oerhört mycket energi av dem. Den tiden och kraften togs ifrån deras föräldraskap. Deras närvaro för mig blev bristfällig. Jag var 10 år och kunde se deras börda, samtidigt som jag själv bar på en djup längtan efter deras vuxna närvaro och stöd. Jag kunde ha blivit en bråkstake för att få vuxenvärldens uppmärksamhet men jag valde istället att "adoptera" en mamma. Vår granne tant Britta tog jag till mig som en extramamma. I vått och torrt ställde hon upp för mig. Hon fanns där alltid som ett känslomässigt stöd. Jag blev omplåstrad när jag hade slagit mig och det var till Britta jag gick efter skolan och åt mellanmål. Kärleken mellan oss växte. Vi behöll kontakten i alla år och i vintras kunde jag gratulera min älskade tant Britta på hennes 80-årsdag.

Som alla barn och ungdomar behövde jag vuxna som vägvisare även när jag själv skulle kliva in i vuxenlivet. Jag hade med mig insikten om hur lätt barn och ungdomar känner sig svikna och övergivna, men saknade en komplett bild av hur man skall finnas till för barnen. På mitt eget unika sätt, med hela min närvaro och med min stora kärlek fanns jag där för mina barn. Det blev en självklarhet att sätta dem i första rum i alla lägen och jag pressade undan mina egna behov. Jag var ankaret för barnen och i familjelivet. Vid ett par tillfälle under barnens uppväxt hamnade alla familjemedlemmar i en djup kris. Tryggheten hängde på en skör tråd. Någon var tvungen att kliva fram och agera. Trots att även jag befann mig i kris, precis som den övriga familjen, kände jag att jag var tvungen att lägga undan mina behov av stöd för att kunna föra den förlista familjen framåt och ut ur krisen.

Jag var skild från barnens pappa när jag fann kärleken och blev förblindad. Jag hängav mig totalt i denna relation till en partner och trodde att kärleken skulle övervinna allt. Även de svårigheter som jag till sist insåg existerade i vårt destruktiva förhållande. Jag upplevde att jag var ansvarig också för detta förhållande och gjorde allt vad jag förmådde i relationen till honom. Det kändes som om jag var på väg att drunkna varje gång ondskans våg sköljde över mig och drog mig ner till havets botten. Men varje gång fann jag åter kraft att stiga upp till ytan och en dag kom uppvaknandet. Jag insåg att jag behövde finnas till för någon annan än för min partner. Jag behövde finnas till för mig själv. Älska mig själv mjukt och passionerat. Värna och stå upp för mina egna behov. Och finnas till för mig själv i både nöd och lust.

Våren kom med ett vägskäl som krävde ett beslut från mig. Valet mellan liv och död, mellan att fortsätta kämpa eller att börja leva. Leva var att följa min egen inre röst. Fortsätta kämpa innebar att göra det som jag trodde förväntades av mig. Det fanns ögonblick då jag hellre önskade att dö än att behöva göra det valet. Döden hägrade som en längtansfull horisont efter en lång vandring i öknen. Döden kändes som en svalkande dryck i den heta sommarnatten. Men jag gav livet en chans. Jag gav mig själv en ny chans. Jag hade fått livet som en gåva och den hade jag en längtan efter att förvalta och njuta av.

I fem dagar befann jag mig i skärgården. Jag mötte havet, naturen, träden, åkrarna, solen och himlen. Allt bjöd upp mig till att utforska den djupa närvaron. Redan från första kvällen hörde jag rösterna som kom från naturen. Träden och åkrarna pockade på min uppmärksamhet och viskade i mitt öra. Mjukt och lent talade de till mig. Trots att jag lyssnade uppmärksamt förmådde jag inte att förstå deras språk. Deras röster bar på en varm kärleksfull stämma. Jag gav inte upp med att försöka lyssna och förstå vad de ville säga mig. Jag blev som ett barn på nytt. Ett samspel uppstod mellan naturen, åkrarna, träden, havet och mig. Jag kastades in i ett tillstånd där jag blev den sommarlovslediga flickan. Jag cyklade och fann en öde ladugård. Stannade upp. Ett tjatter av röster började ljuda inom mig. De talade myndigt och stabilt ..... Det är farligt, tänk om, får man lov ....., och så dök det upp en annan röst som började bubbla inom mig .... jag vill....... på upptäcktsfärd .... leka ....utforska.......... Plötsligt hade fötterna burit iväg med mig och jag befann mig mitt ute på bjälken i ladugården. Hjärtat dunkade hårt. Tankar på vad som skulle kunna hända for runt som raketer i mitt huvud. Samtidigt kunde jag inte förneka att jag sköljdes med i en porlande extas. En stillsam vildhet växte inom mig. Jag hade släppt taget och ingenting höll mig tillbaka. Frihetens längtan hade vaknat till liv. Trots min höjdskräck stod jag ute på ladugårdsbjälken och visste att kärleken till livet skulle bära mig hela vägen över bjälken. Väl framme skrattade jag så högt att mitt gurglande skratt nådde ända upp till himlen och fångades upp av de mjuka sockervaddslika molnen.

Utanför ladugården bjöd gräset mig en vila. Jag lade mig i de mjuka gröna stråna och lät mina ögon beskåda de vackra sommarmolnen där mina skratt dansade till Abbas Dancing Queen. Jag kände mig fri och levande. Varenda cell i min kropp vibrerade av vällust och njutning. Den mjuka brisen smekte min kropp, och solen bäddade in mig i en skön värme. Som en fulländad älskogsakt eggade livet upp mig till total hängivenhet och passion. Naturen viskade mjukt i mitt öra "Rinella, förstår du nu vem du är och vad du är ämnad att göra i det här livet?"

Här i skärgården fann jag utrymme till leken som tillät mig att utforska min egen inre puls tillsammans med naturens röster. Jag fann mitt Sanna Jag som är att vara i njutning och lekfullhet. Mitt Sanna Jag är att vara tätt sammanlänkad med livet och dess puls. Jag behöver få bejaka alla skiftningar och kliva ur formen av måsten som vi människor har skapat. Jag har känt mig fastkedjad. Om nätterna har jag länge lyssnat till rasslet av måstenas alla bojor. Vuxenhetens allvar gick för länge sedan överstyr. Jag var nära att drunkna i allt allvar. Skrattets gurglande läte hade nästan slocknat. Axlarna var tyngda av livets alla måsten och jag släpade fram min kropp med tunga hasande steg. Men inom mig har det alltid brunnit en låga som kommer ur en okänd längtan efter att vara och leva som ett feminint väsen.

Så där låg jag på den smutsiga bryggan i min vita sommarklänning. Något nytt föddes inom mig i detta ögonblick och det var dags att ta ett beslut. Nu fanns det bara ett enda val för mig och det var att kasta mig utför livets klippa i tillit till att det bär mig, såsom det alltid har gjort. Jag valde att leva livet. Jag hade återvunnit mitt Sanna Jag. Hand i hand vandrar jag nu med livet. I nöd och lust. Tills döden skiljer oss åt.

Rinella Grahn är utbildad konstvetare och friskvårdsterapeut. Uppvuxen i ett flerspråkigt hem. Som åttaåring lämnade familjen Japan för att flytta till Sverige. Under skoltiden blev hon berövad sina två modersmål italienska och japanska, en traumatisk upplevelse som ledde till att hon förlorade sin glädje för språk och kommunikation. 2012 fann hon tillbaka till sin röst och sitt språk. Rinella är redo att möta världen med sin föreläsning om hur hon hittade tillbaka till språket, identiteten och rösten. Ytterligare en spännande erfarenhet av språk fick Rinella när hon 2013 arbetade som projektledare i ett filmprojekt för ungdomar med grava språkstörningar.

rinella@rinella.se

A Tribute

to

a Sensual Woman

Roberta A. Creeron

November 27, 1953-
January 5, 2014

In the Introduction, I mentioned the phone call I had with Roberta Creeron as one of the reasons this project happened. Her life ended unexpectedly, a few hours after our phone call. It seems fitting to share a few words about her as we bring this book to a close.

Roberta was a passionate, sensual woman who deeply cared about people. She was the type of woman who would ask questions and sincerely want to know why you thought and felt that way about an issue and about life. People loved her and sometimes feared her. She asked questions that were curious, loving and "inappropriate", the kind of questions that most people would shy away from because it would draw attention to the elephant in the room that no one wanted to see. She wasn't afraid to stir things up and the funny thing is that most of the time she didn't even know she was stirring things up. She just asked the questions with innocence and then wondered why it upset people. She had a voice and she wasn't afraid to use it.

Our last conversation on the last day of her life (an example of the power of connection, following our desires and listening to our intuition):

Roberta sent me a text with an SOS: "Help! Is there any way that we can talk on the phone today?" Roberta had lost her job. She wasn't feeling well physically. The weather was extremely cold on that day in January 2014 and she felt isolated. There had been a series of friends and family with illness and death over the last few months. She had experienced a wave of disappointments and she felt lost. She reached out to me for support and uplifting words. She wanted to infuse herself with some positivity at a time when she was spirally down emotionally and had lost hope. She reached out for CONNECTION.

It had been six months since we had talked on the phone, both of us busy with building businesses and careers and immersed in the relationships we had with local people. I was in California. Roberta was in Maryland. We talked for an hour and shared deep, vulnerable words and feelings. We had been friends for 25 years and it was easy to pick up where we left off.

I was in a deep exploration around Sensuality and the connection to Power and Money and Sexuality. I shared the things I was learning about myself and that I wanted to lead a Heal My Voice project around Sensuality. Her last words to me were about the Sensual Voices project. She told me it was an important subject and it was time. She had just finished watching the film, *The Sessions*, starring the actress Helen Hunt. She said, "You have to have this conversation. If anyone can create a safe space for women, it's you! Write stories from the body, about the body. Write about desire and sex. Talk about orgasm and connection and desire. Don't wait."

We ended the conversation by making plans to see each other a month later when I would be in Baltimore. She wanted to write a story in this book and share her own journey of sensuality. A few days later, I received a call from Roberta's sister and learned the news that Roberta had died a few hours after our conversation from an abdominal aneurism.

*****

Roberta was a renaissance woman who lived her life with authenticity, sensuality and wide-eyed wonder. She inspired and loved so many people throughout her life. That was her sensual expression: LOVE.

She pushed against the norms in life and experienced a wide range of sensations and experiences while still trying to fit in. Born in New York City to a large Catholic family she traveled as a young adult to San Francisco where she was a member of the Unification Church, a "Moonie." She was drawn to the messages of anti-Communism, pro-America and the words Love, Unite, Forgive, which were a fit for Roberta who was a seeker and a woman who loved community. She married, gave birth to two daughters and divorced her husband who later became a famous baseball game announcer. Like many of us, she tried to fit into a "normal life" with a big personality that called her to live and experience everything.

Roberta defined herself as a heterosexual woman who also fell in love with a woman and lived with her for six years. When Roberta tried to make sense of this, one of her daughters said, "Mom, I think you just love who you love." That was Roberta.

She loved making life beautiful. Cooking delicious meals for friends, Creating flower arrangements and decorating her home. She surrounded herself with beautiful things and beautiful people. She was the epitome of generosity.

I miss her presence in my life deeply.

*****

I end with a few words from Roberta:

An email sent to me after an evening gathering with Roberta, a friend, Kater Leatherman and me:

Yesterday was a treasure. Thank you for all of it. What a comfort our friendship is, a beautiful, downy "throw" pillow on the sofa of my life.

You are a brave loving soul, and all the paths in your life are converging in your quest to bring more love and peace into the world now. Enjoy the journey. Reap the blessings.

One of her desires from an affirmation in her journal:

Thank you Father for my beloved,
A magnificent, mind energy
A mirroring of me in the masculine,
Healthy, robust,
Blending spirituality with intelligence and
tenderness and unselfishness
Who is nurturing
And curious
And hilarious
And perfect for me now.

And an article about life that inspired her.
This is the way she lived her life:

Written By Regina Brett, 90 years old, of The
Plain Dealer,_Cleveland , Ohio

"To celebrate growing older, I once wrote the
44 lessons life taught
me. It is the most-requested column I've ever
written. My odometer
rolled over to 90 in August, so here is the
column once more:"

1. Life isn't fair, but it's still good.
2. When in doubt, just take the next small step.
3. Life is too short to waste time hating anyone.

4. Your job won't take care of you when you are sick. Your friends and
parents will. Stay in touch.

5. Pay off your credit cards every month.

6. You don't have to win every argument. Agree to disagree.

7. Cry with someone. It's more healing than crying alone.

8. It's OK to get angry with God. He can take it.

9. Save for retirement starting with your first paycheck.

10. When it comes to chocolate, resistance is futile.

11. Make peace with your past so it won't screw up the present.

12. It's OK to let your children see you cry.

13. Don't compare your life to others. You have no idea what their
journey is all about.

14. If a relationship has to be a secret, you shouldn't be in it.

15. Everything can change in the blink of an eye. But don't worry; God
never blinks.

16. Take a deep breath. It calms the mind

17. Get rid of anything that isn't useful, beautiful or joyful.

18. Whatever doesn't kill you really does make you stronger.

19. It's never too late to have a happy childhood. But the second one

is up to you and no one else.

20. When it comes to going after what you love in life, don't take no

for an answer.

21. Burn the candles, use the nice sheets, wear the fancy lingerie.

Don't save it for a special occasion. Today is special.

22. Over prepare, then go with the flow.

23. Be eccentric now. Don't wait for old age to wear purple.

24. No one is in charge of your happiness but you.

25. Frame every so-called disaster with these words "In five years,

will this matter?".

26. Always choose life.

27 Forgive everyone everything.

28. What other people think of you is none of your business.

29. Time heals almost everything. Give time, time.

30. However good or bad a situation is, it will change.

31. Don't take yourself so seriously. No one else does.

32. Believe in miracles.

33. God loves you because of who God is, not because of anything you

did or didn't do.

34. Don't audit life. Show up and make the most of it now.

35. Growing old beats the alternative -- dying young.

36. Your children get only one childhood.

37. All that truly matters in the end is that you loved.

38. Get outside every day. Miracles are waiting everywhere.

39. If we all threw our problems in a pile and saw everyone else's,

we'd grab ours back.

40. Envy is a waste of time. You already have all you need.

41. The best is yet to come.

42. No matter how you feel, get up, dress up, and show up.

43. Yield.

44. Life isn't tied with a bow, but it's still a gift.

Roberta A. Creeron

November 27, 1953-
January 5, 2014

Heal My Voice <u>*Mission*</u>

www.healmyvoice.org

Join us in our mission to help each woman discover her voice:

Heal My Voice empowers and supports women and girls globally to heal, reclaim their voice and step into greater leadership in their lives and in the world.

Your Voice Matters!

Thank you to our Sponsors

Sponsors

Mary K. Baxter
http://dramaticadventure.com/

Cassandra Herbert
http://www.zestandharmonycouns
eling.com/

Ellen Koronet
http://LNKcreative.com

Marie Ek Lipanovska
http://www.healmyvoicesweden.c
om/

Monisha Mittal
http://www.yourinnerease.com/

Karen Porter
http://www.mamaporter.com/

Amber Scott
http://truevoice.com/

Jamie Dee Schiffer
http://www.a-passionate-life.com/

Beth Terrence
http://www.bethterrence.com/

Kathleen Nelson Troyer
http://kathleennelsontroyer.com

Heal My Voice Book Series

http://healmyvoice.org/

Fearless Voices:
True Stories by Courageous
Women
2012

Empowered Voices:
True Stories by Awakened
Women
2012

Inspired Voices:
True Stories by Visionary Women
2013

Harmonic Voices:
True Stories by Women on the
Path to Peace
2014

Tender Voices:
True Stories by Women on a
Journey of Love
2014

Feminine Voices:
True Stories by Women
Transforming Leadership
2014

Sensual Voices:
True Stories by Women Exploring
Connection and Desire
2015

Heal My Voice Sweden

http://www.healmyvoicesweden.com/

Värdefulla Röster
2013

Frigörande Röster
2014